CAN YOU HEAR GOD NOW?

This book does what its' title advertises: It provides a roadmap for a journey into a deeper relationship with the God who created us. Based on careful study of the Bible, and her own experience, coupled with input from a carefully designed survey returned by over 600 recipients, Sue Roberts has written what may be one of the most useful recent books on Christian faith and living. Each chapter combines Scripture with carefully selected stories to offer clear and practical ideas of steps along a journey toward God. The questions at the end of the chapters are among the most thoughtful of any book I have read, and can be very effectively used for study and application by individuals or groups. This is a book very much worth reading, studying, and applying.

> — **Col. Alexander Shine** (Retired Army), lay leader for
> military chapels and Officer Christian Fellowship.

"Some people hear from God and some people go years without recognizing his voice. Susan Roberts lays a strong biblical foundation for establishing effective communication with God. Her stories are credible and provide inspiring examples of God's interactions with normal and sane people. Her book brings acuity to our ears."

> — **Dr. Marshall Shelley**, Director of the Doctor
> of Ministry program, Denver Seminary

"For most of us God's voice seems silent (Psalm 22:2) or at best very quiet (1 Kings 19:12). Yet when we step out in faith upon what we feel is God's direction, we will later see in hindsight that God was really guiding us. This book provides many real examples of such godly communications and guidance."

> — **Dr. Edmond W. Holroyd, III**, (retired)
> federal scientist and graduate school professor

"When God makes a promise, you can take it to the bank. Jesus promised every believer that they would hear the voice of God when He said, "My sheep hear my voice" (John 10:27). How else can we know that we are doing God's will and walking in His plan for our lives? Based firmly on biblical truth, *Can You Hear God Now* presents practical steps to enter into an interactive relationship with God—where we talk to Him, and yes, He talks to us. Author Sue Roberts includes stories from throughout history of believers who heard God's voice and walked in His will. Roberts shows that when we pay attention, listening for the voice of our Heavenly Father, this life becomes an exciting adventure."

— **Dr. Craig von Buseck**, Editor, Inspiration.org

"Sue digs deeply into God's word, and freely shares her heart, her struggles and her insights. We were both challenged and blessed as we dove into the wealth that her book offers. It is evident that God still speaks today."

—**Jim and Pat Burdick**, readers

"This is not a book of preachy practices but simple stories from people of all ages and stages showing that God is here and we can hear Him when we listen. *Can You Hear God Now* challenged and encouraged me to enjoy God's abundant blessings which await me when I listen, trust in and rely on Him."

— **Laura Padgett**, author, speaker

"I got goosebumps when I read the stories. They showed me how God had been speaking to me and I haven't noticed. Inspiring. A must read."

— **Michelle Arbuckle**, reader

CAN YOU HEAR GOD NOW?

*How to Journey to a Deeper
Relationship with God*

SUSAN ROBERTS

NASHVILLE

NEW YORK • LONDON • MELBOURNE • VANCOUVER

CAN YOU HEAR GOD NOW?
How to Journey to a Deeper Relationship with God

© 2019 SUSAN ROBERTS

Published in New York, New York, by Morgan James Publishing. Morgan James is a trademark of Morgan James, LLC. www.MorganJamesPublishing.com

ISBN 978-1-64279-236-2 paperback
ISBN 978-1-64279-237-9 eBook
Library of Congress Control Number: 2018910391

Cover Design by:
Rachel Lopez
www.r2cdesign.com

Interior Design by:
Bonnie Bushman
The Whole Caboodle Graphic Design

Editing by:
Deb Hall, The Write Insight
www.TheWriteInsight.com

In an effort to support local communities, raise awareness and funds, Morgan James Publishing donates a percentage of all book sales for the life of each book to Habitat for Humanity Peninsula and Greater Williamsburg.

Get involved today! Visit
www.MorganJamesBuilds.com

To God, my empowerer
To Perry, my encourager
To many others, my enablers
I couldn't have done this without you.
Thank-you

TABLE OF CONTENTS

FOREWORD

I have long wished for a red phone that would sit on my desk, available at any time for those key moments when I really wanted God's input on a major decision. The chance to hear God's voice like I hear my wife's or that of my close friends would be so great! But so far, neither Ma Bell nor Amazon have been able to provide the specs for such a device.

Thus, the need for a book like the one you hold in your hands. When Sue Roberts told me that she was going to write a book that sought to address the topic of how we hear from God, I immediately wished her good luck! (Or should I say, good providence!) Of all the subjects she could have chosen to address, this is one of the most challenging, elusive, divisive, and multi-faceted. The need for guidance on this aspect of the Christian life is clear. But who in their right mind would choose to walk into such a lion's den? I commend Sue for tackling the challenge!

One part of the Christian world is inhabited by those who believe that anyone can hear audibly from God at almost any time, if they have but the faith and desire. I have known dear brothers and sisters in Christ who claim this as their own experience. But for whatever reason, I have never personally encountered God in this way. I have never heard audibly from God in my sixty-four years on this planet. And if I am to be completely honest, I'm not always sure that those who do claim this experience have always had their radios dialed in quite the way they think. But God is God, and He is free to act as He chooses.

I must admit that if God were, in fact, communicating this way, it would leave me feeling a bit like the child on the edge of the playground who never got picked for kickball. My experience, or lack of it, with the voice of God would leave me wondering if there is something wrong with me, or if God doesn't like me as much as He likes those other kids. However, I don't believe it is really a matter of one's standing with God. As Sue highlights, there are many other things to consider. So I remain cautiously open to the possibility.

On the opposite end of the spectrum are those who believe that all revelation of any kind has ceased with the close of the New Testament. Those in this camp would suggest that Scripture, and the New Testament in particular, provide us with all the revelation we need as we make our way through this world. The Montanist debate of the 2nd century settled this debate once and for all, some would claim, and the church has declared a seal on new revelation with the end of the Apostolic era.

Yet in between these camps are the lives of every day, ordinary believers who yearn for some sort of ongoing guidance from the Holy Spirit. They sincerely hope God is still at work answering their prayers as they make decisions both large and small. When God doesn't speak audibly, might there be other ways that God leads and guides His children in the twenty-first century?

The answer of this book is very much in the affirmative as it explores the many non-auditory ways in which God also leads, directs, comforts, and guides His children in the day to day life. Many believers never "hear" from God, yet they have a deep awareness of God's ongoing involvement in their lives.

Sue Roberts has done a yeoman's job at delving into the nuances of this larger conversation. She has sought to be biblically grounded in every aspect of the discussion. She has written with respect and interpersonal sensitivity to a wide variety of voices. She has done her homework and research. And she has demonstrated that the answer to her title question is not one-size-fits-all.

Thus, I commend Sue's book to you, not as the last word on this subject, but as a wonderful contribution to a tough topic that will give you much to consider and incorporate during your days on this earth. Someday, we will be able to walk and talk with God again like Adam and Eve did in the garden. In the meantime, our loving, living Lord might well want to meet you in some of the very same ways that Sue has outlined in this work. It might not be through a red phone on your desk, but it can still help you know that God is with you as you seek to live a faithful life full of wisdom and discernment.

—**Dr. John R. Martz**, Pastor (retired)
Arvada Covenant Church, Arvada, CO

INTRODUCTION

I approached the river. The water was swift and strong. "You want me to do what, Lord?" I asked. "Step in the river?" "But, I'm afraid. I can't swim. I'll be swept away and lose control, and I might even die. I'm safer here on the bank. I don't need to cross. Everything I need is here."

But Jesus answered me, saying, "I am with you, and will never leave you. My strength is made perfect in your weakness. I uphold you with my right hand. Come. I will make the way. Come. Let's go together. I have so much to show you on the other side of the river! A promised land awaits."

But, Jesus …

What is the river before you? Is it beginning a relationship with God that you aren't sure about? Does He even exist? What does He want from you? What do you have to do? Is God truly there for you and will He make a difference in your life? Can you count on Him? It's scary to turn and begin to follow someone you don't even know. This isn't just a step, but a leap of faith.

Does stepping in the river mean pursing a deeper relationship with Jesus? Do you need to step out of your comfort zone and respond to His call? Are there things He's trying to change in you, yet you struggle and resist? How can you be sure His way is the best way? The status quo is safer, and you can serve God there in your own way.

Perhaps you are already in the river, struggling in your own strength to keep your head above water. The cares of this world are overwhelming. You are being swept along by the current, barely able to cope. You are desperately looking for solid ground or something to cling to. You are calling, "Where are you, God? Help me!"

The priests, leading Israel to the promised land, were carrying the ark of the covenant. They approached the Jordan River which was at flood stage. God had told them He would cut off the water flowing downstream and make it "stand up in a heap" so they could get across (Joshua 3:13). Sure.

Yet, they trusted God implicitly, heading to the water without hesitation. They maneuvered the heavy ark down the steep, slippery bank. The Bible tells us that *when their feet touched the water* the river stopped flowing and they were able to cross on dry land. Did they doubt or say, "What if?" Did they have a contingency plan? They didn't stop at the top and wait for God to work before heading down the slippery slope. The way was opened *when* they stepped into the river.

We can sit on the banks of our rivers hesitating, waiting for God to show up. We can make our own plans to get across. Maybe we can build a bridge over the river. But God says our plans won't succeed without Him (Proverbs 19:21). We can struggle by our own strength to battle the currents. But I believe Jesus tells us "Have faith. I love you and have promised to take care of you and guide you. I will help you. You must walk by faith, not by sight" (2 Corinthians 5:7 NKJV). God opens the way, but He doesn't show us until we commit. Then He will make our way secure one step at a time. He is our rock, the one we can cling to. Walk with Him. Your promised land is ahead. Step in the river.

There are new, exciting things ahead for you! Come and see. Did you know God loves you just as you are? Did you know God wants a relationship with you where He can talk to you? Are you eager to see what He has in store for you? Are you curious to see what God is doing in the lives of others?

I've begun my own journey of discovering how to listen to God and how to discern if God really is speaking to me. The Bible has convinced me that Jesus has made the way for us to become friends with God so we can talk to Him. He also will talk to us. Friends converse. I've learned a lot about my relationship with

Jesus—what He expects of me and what I can expect of Him. This has begun a new level of spiritual intimacy. I'm excited to share with you what I've learned.

Reading, researching and studying Scripture has provided a foundation for my journey. In addition, I've been inspired by numerous stories people have sent to me about their God encounters. God is most definitely speaking into the lives of His people today and it is amazing how much He cares for each detail of our lives. When we expect Him to speak and learn how to hear Him, we enter an incredible intimate relationship with Almighty God.

At the end of each chapter, optional thought questions have been provided that can help you think about some of the key points of the chapters, or help you discuss the concepts with others in a group. In addition, some extra Scripture passages or another activity is provided.

Come with me on a journey to learn how God speaks, and how to better hear Him. I'm certain this is a journey worth taking. A promised land of excitement and fulfillment awaits those who by faith will step in this river.

Chapter One

ARE YOU CRAZY?

Are people who hear God mentally ill?

Listen and hear my voice; pay attention and hear what I say.
(Isaiah 28:23)

Campus was abuzz with rumors and speculation. A beloved yet controversial professor was scheduled to speak in chapel. He had dropped a few teasers in his classes, so anticipation was high. Chapel was packed.

His topic of the day was "The Silence of God." The premise? God no longer speaks today. He has become silent. Do you see prayers answered and miracles? Do you see revival? Do you see sinful nations and people being punished? The wicked prosper. The virtuous suffer. Where is God? We are on our own to figure it out.

In those days the word of the Lord was rare; there were not many visions.
(1 Samuel 3:1)

"The days are coming," declares the Sovereign LORD, "when I will send a famine through the land—not a famine of food or a thirst for water, but a famine of hearing the words of the Lord. People will stagger from sea to sea and wander from north to east, searching for the word of the Lord, but they will not find it."
(Amos 8:11–12)

The timer light on the back wall of the chapel flashed. In defiance, the professor ignored it. "I'm not done yet," he asserted. The dean of the faculty, behind him on the stage, stood up and handed him a note. He let it slip to the floor, as he continued speaking. Students hung on his every word. Some self-wise students smiled smugly, nodding their heads in all-knowing agreement. It was about time somebody spoke the truth. But others shifted uncomfortably in their seats. This was not right. Of course God is still around. Of course He answers prayer. Of course He speaks. We haven't entered an age of silence from God!

After the service, students started talking. The debates were heated. Bibles appeared. The majority shared stories of recent times when God had spoken, answered prayer and performed miracles. The discussions continued far into the evening. The professor himself was experiencing a dark time of God's silence, but he hoped that in examining this, there would be answers. He wanted to shake up the apathy. He wanted to see evidence of God's work and confirm that God will pursue a relationship with people.

If you had been there, how would you have argued? Would you have nodded your head and said, "Yes, God is silent these days," or would you have built the case for His presence, His personal relationship with us, and His acts on our behalf? Do you have evidence to share?

The people of Israel turned to idols and their own self-sufficiency because they thought God had long been silent. Instead of seeking Him and remembering what He had done, they ceased to fear Him (Isaiah 57: 10–11). Does our society act this way also?

I received more than six hundred replies to a survey I sent out asking people if they believe God speaks today, to whom He speaks and how He speaks. How do we hear Him? How do we know it's God? People from twenty-five states, six foreign countries and various religious backgrounds, age groups, and occupations responded. The specific results are catalogued in the appendix.

Ninety-six percent of the people who responded believe that God does speak today. In fact, most agreed He will speak to anyone and everyone, though people might not recognize His voice. Many indicated that they have personally heard from God at some time.

The evidence of people who believe God has interacted with them has been established in the survey results. If only a few people had responded, the reports could be considered coincidental, or skeptics could say that folks have been misinformed. However, the sheer volume of those who have heard God speak to them in a variety of ways, in several different kinds of situations, validates God's desire to communicate with us and inspires us to pay attention.

But there are skeptics out there. The resistance to the idea of God speaking is prevalent. Even in the light of the evidence, there are those, including religious people, who raise their eyebrows or guffaw when someone says that they have heard the voice of God. The following comment by an atheist who thinks Christians hearing God need professional intervention, sums up the attitude that many have. "If someone said a toaster was sending them life advice, we'd say they needed help. If they said a unicorn told them to run for president, we'd laugh them off. If we don't have the same reactions when people substitute in the Christian God, it's only because we're so used to hearing it."[1]

Equating hearing God's voice to mental illness is not that farfetched. Joy Behar created a sensation on her TV show *The View*[2] when she attacked Vice President Mike Pence's comment that he had heard God speak and that God tells him what to do. She suggested that hearing voices is mental illness. However, many of our presidents have said they have heard from God. Washington, Lincoln, FDR, Carter, Clinton, and Obama have all made that claim.[3]

Dr. T. M. Luhrmann, a psychological anthropologist at Stanford University did a ten-year study of what she describes as "experientially oriented evangelicals,"[4] trying to determine if their claim of hearing God's voice did mean that they were mentally ill. Her results were published in her book: *When God Talks Back: Understanding the American Evangelical Relationship with God.* She surmised, "When you talk to God, we call it prayer. When God talks to you, we call it schizophrenia."[5] Dr. Luhrmann noted that schizophrenics hear continual debilitating voices that include destructive insults, sneers, and jibes. People who hear God report an empowering, quiet voice of love and peace, and feel an intimate relationship with Him. Dr. Luhrmann concluded that people who hear God speak are not mentally ill.[6]

The ridicule surrounding people who hear from God, caused some who responded to the survey to be reluctant to share their personal experiences. They didn't want them "out there" for public scrutiny. However, Nora shared this story.

"Years ago, my husband was teaching at the U.S. Air Force Academy where they have a beautiful chapel. I am Catholic. Although the Catholic Chapel downstairs is lovely, the upstairs main chapel with its blue windows is spectacular. I sat there to admire the beauty and God spoke to me. Later I told a friend, who said that was nice but not to tell others. I was offended because I knew he didn't believe that it really happened to me."

J. Wallace Warner, a Senior Fellow at the Colson Center, wrote a commentary about hearing God as a response to the vogue negativity that surfaced following Joy Behar's comments.[7] He noted that when people say, "God spoke to me," they rarely mean that God spoke to them audibly, although God occasionally does do that. God typically speaks in a still, small voice—an impression in one's mind. He also speaks through other means such as the Bible and nature. He might use teachers, preachers, family, and friends to report His message. He might even use dreams or send angels. Later chapters in this book will examine ways God might speak to us. To hear Him, we need to expect Him to speak and then pay attention. Paying attention is the first great act of worship,[8] where we show due reverence to God and focus on His attributes. This opens the door to communicating with Him. Yet, in our busy lives this is often neglected.

> "We must admit that we forget our God, that we do not notice our Creator, that we remain distracted. That, like Augustine, we must confess, 'You were with me, but I was not with you.'"[9]

I believe, based on biblical accounts and the evidence presented by my survey, that each of us can develop an intimate conversational relationship with God. In order to do so, we need to lay aside our inhibitions and prejudices, stop running and start looking. When we allow God into our lives and learn to recognize His voice, we will be surprised at the variety of ways He will communicate with us every day. Friends converse. The purpose of this book is to help us on our journey to friendship with God.

Look for Him. Listen to Him. Expect Him to show up. Be open to whatever means God wishes to use to talk to you. "Today, if you hear His voice, do not harden your hearts" (Hebrews 3: 7–8). With a ready heart and a right spirit, listen to God. "Speak, Lord, for Your servant is listening." (1 Samuel 3:10 AMPC) He has things to tell you and show you.

Open my eyes so I can see what you show me of your miracle-wonders
(Psalm 119:18 MSG).

——•◆ *Stop and Refresh* ◆•——

1. Read Joshua 1:1–10. What are some things God told Joshua and the people of Israel to do to prepare for their journey to the promised land? Do any of these apply today?

2. Read the introduction. What "rivers" in your life pose a threat to you?

3. Do you feel like God is silent today? Why? Do you have evidence that He isn't?

4. What is your reaction when someone tells you they have heard from God?

5. Have you had an experience where God has interacted with you? Have you told anyone? How did they react? Are you willing to share this with others now?

Chapter Two

I'M BEING FOLLOWED

God pursues us not wanting anyone to perish.

Where can I go from your Spirit?
Where can I flee from your presence?
(Psalm 139:7)

If God is speaking, to whom does He speak? Are only Christians or the very religious privy to hearing from God, or will He talk to everyone? The majority of people who answered the survey agreed that God will talk to everyone, but they might not recognize His voice. Is this true? In addition to answering the questions, many survey responders included captivating stories about God interacting with them. Some of the most fascinating replies came from those who did not yet have a relationship with God. In retrospect, they have realized God was caring for them, protecting them and calling them in remarkable ways, even before they knew who He was. A friend told me this story.

"It was 3:00 a.m. I sat in my car in a church parking lot wishing someone would attack me or ram me with their car. I was done. I saw no reason to go on living. A few days earlier, I had tried to take my life with an overdose, but in my naïveté, the excess vitamin C and aspirin did nothing. As I looked out across the valley, I saw a huge lighted cross on the side of a hill. 'Okay, God,' I said, 'If you are real, you have two weeks to reveal yourself and show me a reason to live.'

I had grown up in an abusive home with physical and mental abuse as well as constant fighting. I avoided being home, where everything I did was ridiculed. We went to church because that was expected of upstanding citizens, but no one there talked about a personal relationship with Jesus. By high school, my self-esteem hit the bottom. I developed acne and gained weight. My lack of focus in school netted mediocre grades, so when I applied for colleges, I received rejection after rejection. This despair brought me to the parking lot.

I left, drove home and climbed in my bedroom window, telling no one what had happened. A few days later, a brother-in-law took me to lunch and suggested I apply for Boise State since he had family there. I applied and was accepted. I flew there by myself, was picked up by people I did not know, and dropped off at the dorm with my one suitcase. I was lonely and fearful, but I somehow sensed God was with me. I took long walks, talking to a God I did not know. His reality for me was confirmed when I discovered a large lighted cross on a hillside in Boise also.

When I went home for Christmas break, a friend's mom suggested I join her daughter at a community college which offered the strong language skills I was lacking. It also offered work study programs. At work, I met a girl who invited me to her church where I heard the message of a God who loves me and wants a relationship with me. I spent every moment I could at the church, attending every service, and even doing my homework in the empty sanctuary. The pastor and his wife took me under their wings and mentored me. I turned my life over to Jesus, and for the first time felt peace. Eventually, others in my family began attending the church with me. They turned their lives over to God also.

When I look back and see how God reached down to save me—literally—I am so convinced of His reality, His love, and His interaction with me. I didn't seek Him in the beginning, but He found me and took control of my life."

God does save us in miraculous ways, orchestrating circumstances and putting us just where we need to be to find Him. He brings people into our lives and speaks to us through them. He protects us from ourselves and the evil around us. My friend, Glory, shared an amazing story about how God reached down to save her from her destructive situation. He had a plan for her life.

Glory grew up in an abusive, legalistic home. Her family attended church, but all she heard was condemnation. To escape, she turned to alcohol and drugs. She was in such despair that she tried to commit suicide by taking pills, but vomited and couldn't keep them down. Determined to try again, she decided to step in front of a bus. Somehow, some way, she ended up on the opposite side of the street, sitting on the sidewalk. She has no idea how she got there. She now believes she was rescued by an angel.

To escape her devastating home life, she left at seventeen and married a man who also turned out to be abusive. Her pastor told her it was her fault because she wasn't a good wife. Her downward spiral continued. She became addicted to cocaine and dropped to eighty pounds, barely able to function. Again, she tried suicide by overdosing on cocaine, but her mom showed up in time to save her.

A few weeks later on a Friday, she attended a youth rally and heard the song "Amado Mio," translated as "My Savior." God spoke to her and said that He was the only one who could save her. Two days later, on Sunday, the pastor of her parents' church laid hands on her and prayed for her. She fell backwards and stayed on the floor for twenty minutes. When she stood up, she was a new person— cleaned and healed. Cocaine no longer had a hold on her. It wasn't immediate, but God began to orchestrate circumstances in her life that provided for her rehabilitation. She met a man who loved her unconditionally and showed her what God's love was like. She began a ministry for abused women and addicts and has a vision to open a center for the victims of domestic violence. God intervened in her life dramatically, saving her from evil and giving her a purpose and calling, even using the devastation in her life to accomplish something good. God protected Glory from her own poor choices and the evil that surrounded her. She is so amazed that in His love, He was looking out for her, even when she didn't care.

Annette also made poor choices and found herself in dangerous situations. She too is grateful that God protected her from harm and reached out to save her.

Annette recounted, "I was all dressed up to go to a job interview. My ride fell through, but I didn't want to miss my appointment, so I walked six miles in the snow, wind and cold. By the time I made it to my appointment, it turned out the position wasn't even available, so I headed back home—six miles again, in the cold, wind and snow. It was dusk and soon would be dark. When I passed by a filling station, a man putting gas in his car offered me a ride. I took it. He took a detour, suggesting we go out for drinks first. I had no way of escape. I ordered a non-alcoholic drink, but he changed my order and kept drinks coming. I made an excuse to go to the restroom, thinking I could climb out a window, but there were no windows. I pleaded with him to take me home. By now it was dark. We went outside to the parking lot where we were alone. He had a cast on his arm, and he could have hit me with it. He locked me in the car, and when I reached over to unlock my side, I saw the button had been removed. Now I started to panic. 'Surely someone will walk out and see me struggling to get out of the car,' I thought. For some unknown reason, he unlocked the car and quietly let me out. He pulled away and I was on my own to get home in the dark—no cell phone, no money, no ride. I looked up and saw a friend of mine from high school. He took me straight home. I believe God put him there. He doesn't know how he saved me that night, but God used him after I had set myself up for failure. I have many stories like that as I look back on my wild life before Jesus.

However, God pursued me. My college roommate told me about Jesus, but for six months, I resisted. Finally, in exasperation, I agreed to join her at a Christian coffee house. I heard the gospel, and the Holy Spirit audibly called my name. I responded and became a believer. The next morning, I lit a bonfire on my back porch in my barbecue grill and burned everything that I felt did not give God the glory—record albums, letters, photos, memorabilia. I even tried to burn jewelry. I wanted nothing to do with memories of my former life. Nobody told me to do this. I just cleaned house and enjoyed it. I went back to my dorm and read the Bible cover to cover all weekend, fasting and praying. It was an amazing time. I was totally transformed from the inside out."

Those with some Bible knowledge may be familiar with the story of God calling Saul on the road to Damascus in Acts 9. I have been surprised to hear about similar experiences today and realize that they aren't all that uncommon. I've heard several stories from the Middle East about God appearing in dreams or visions to people of different religions. David, who was working with Christian Syrian refugees, went into their small makeshift church gathering of about one hundred people. He was told that everyone in attendance had "seen the vision"—everyone had personally encountered Jesus in a literal sense, by a vision or a visit.

Several years ago, a friend of mine in Hawaii was a follower of the ancient Hawaiian religion. He was driving along a coastal mountain road. In the sky, the sun's rays were streaming from behind a cloud, and a brilliant rainbow arched from the cliffs to the sea. A voice called his name. "Who are you?" he asked. The voice said, "I Am who I Am." He was rather shaken, so he decided to stop at a hotel to collect his bearings. A Gideon Bible had been placed in the room, and for some reason, he began to read it voraciously. God spoke to Him through the Bible and he gave his heart to God, later becoming a minister.

Most of us don't have sensational stories like these, but those of us who know God may look back in our own lives and see how God cared for us and called us to Himself, even before we knew Him. Even if you do not yet have a relationship with God, you may feel a tugging, a vacancy, a sense that God is there.

In his poem, *The Hound of Heaven,* nineteenth century poet Francis Thompson painted a vivid picture of God pursuing us, even when we run from Him.[10] The original language is hard to understand, but the story came alive for me in the poignant YouTube rendition of *The Hound of Heaven, a Modern Adaptation.*[11] The protagonist hears the footsteps of the Hound's pursuit, but runs, thinking the pursuer will require her very life. She indulges in all kinds of pleasures and pursuits looking for fulfillment and happiness but finds no satisfaction. She even tries community service, thinking the good works will fill her void. They don't. Eventually, in despair, she realizes that none of her choices have provided contentment. The Hound continues to follow, though she hurts Him by throwing rocks at Him. With nothing left, she tries to take her own life.

Francis Schaeffer says that in a fallen world, we must be willing to face the fact that however lovingly the gospel is preached, if a man rejects it he will be miserable. It is dark out there.[12] Yes, many run from God and will not listen. They ignore Him and try all sorts of things to fill the void in their lives--that God-shaped hole. Nothing works except God. Augustine said, "You have made us for Yourself, O Lord, and our hearts are restless until they rest in You."[13]

Fortunately, the protagonist in our story finds the compassion, forgiveness and acceptance of the Hound. Yes, she relinquishes her desires and will, but in doing so, finds a life of meaning and purpose in His love and care.

Pat's story illustrates the relentless pursuit of Jesus. Even when we reject Him, He seeks to draw us to Himself.

Pat's Mom, Aldine, sat in a nursing home. Eight years earlier, she had been diagnosed with a serious illness, and at that time was only given six weeks to live. Now, years later she was still alive, but as her health deteriorated, her family could no longer care for her, so she was moved to a nursing home. They would come to visit, but she had reached the point where she didn't know who they were. She could no longer carry on a meaningful conversation.

Aldine had some tough times in her life which had left her bitter and angry. Pat had become a believer in Jesus just a few months before her mother's diagnosis, and she tried to tell her mom about Jesus, but she would get angry and refused to listen. One day while reading the Bible, Pat happened upon the verse from 2 Peter 3:9 which says that it is God's will that none should perish, but that all should come to repentance. That verse encouraged Pat and her husband Jim to pray daily for Aldine's salvation, but they saw no change in her attitude.

One afternoon when Pat and her friend Marlene came to visit Aldine, the nursing staff stopped them. "Your mother didn't have a very good night," they told Pat. "She kept having a nightmare about falling into a deep dark hole and was very frightened." Pat and Marlene hurried to her room. To their surprise Aldine was lucid and cheerful. "Hi, Pat, Hi, Marlene," she said. As they talked, Pat and Marlene asked her if she wanted to accept Jesus as her Savior. Aldine said that she had been asked that as a young teenager but hadn't done it. Now she was ready. About an hour later her clarity ended, and a few days later she passed away. Pat and her husband were greatly comforted to know that Aldine had made a decision to accept Jesus in answer to their years of prayer. God had pursued Aldine even in her bitterness and illness, giving her an alarming dream that prepared her heart, and a moment of lucidity so that she could finally respond to Him.

God does speak to everyone. We have seen how God can break into our lives even when we don't know Him or aren't looking for Him. He is looking for us (Luke 15). He uses all sorts of methods to draw people to Himself, as the stories have illustrated. He even reveals Himself to everyone in His world around us. The book of Romans shows that we all can see God through nature, but we often choose to ignore Him or reinvent Him. "For ever since the world was created, people have seen the earth and sky. Through everything God made, they can clearly see his invisible qualities—his eternal power and divine nature. So they have no excuse for not knowing God" (Romans 1:20 NLT).

We cannot create a God of our own choosing. Understanding who God is and how He works shapes our receptiveness to His voice. If we feel God is angry, demanding and will spoil all our fun, we too will run. If we think He is aloof, uncaring, or shows favoritism, we won't expect Him to interact with us an ordinary person. If we think God expects us to handle life on our own, we won't be looking for His guidance. If He only speaks through His Word, the Bible, then we won't look for Him elsewhere.

Although God interacts with us in many ways, the Bible is our primary source for knowing God, and He will never speak in a way that contradicts it. When we read the Bible, we will truly develop a sense of God's majesty, love, and grace toward us, seeing that He does indeed desire a two-way relationship with each of us and pursues us to establish it. Jesus came to this world to reconcile us to God so that we could communicate with Him. Communication involves both talking (praying) and listening for God to speak. The deeper our relationship with God becomes, the more we know He hears us, and the more we will hear from Him in many ways. But, how do we do that effectively?

Many of us find that talking to and hearing from God is difficult. "Can you hear me now?" This cell phone advertisement underscored the frustration of impeded communication. Do you experience this when you try to communicate with God? I do. When we talk to God in prayer, how do we know He hears us? Sometimes our prayers seem to stop at the ceiling, yet we are told that God hears and answers prayer (Isaiah 65:24). If He speaks to us, how do we know it is God? Is it just our imagination? Is the devil trying to dupe us? We can learn to discern.

Many obstacles impede a clear channel to God's voice, but there are ways that we can clear that channel and learn to listen and follow. Jesus said, "My sheep listen to my voice, I know them, and they follow me" (John 10:27). If we sheep are having a tough time with the listening part, let's fix that. He is pursuing us and has made a way for us to come to Him, but we must respond. He has promised, "If you seek me you will find me, if you seek me with all your heart" (Jeremiah 29:13).

The Lord is good to those whose hope is in him, to the one who seeks him.
(Lamentations 3:25)

——◆ *Stop and Refresh* ◆——

1. Watch the YouTube video: *The Hound of Heaven, A Modern Adaptation at* https://www.youtube.com/watch?v=RXlgz4aBKt8. What impressed you?
2. Share your story of how God pursued you to bring you to Himself. If you do not yet know Him, do you sense He is pursuing you?
3. Do you know someone who needs God? What can you do to point them in His direction?
4. What frustrates you when you try to communicate with God?
5. What is meant by two-way communication? Do you think we can expect this with God? Why or why not?

Chapter Three

THE ULTIMATE GIFT

God's incomparable gift of salvation by grace

"Thanks be to God for His indescribable gift!"
(2 Corinthians 9:15 NKJV)

To figure out why we have so much trouble communicating with God, we need to go back in history—way, way back to the beginning—to see what went wrong. In the beginning, God created the heavens and the earth, and people. As a friend, He walked and talked with Adam and Eve throughout the paradise garden He had created. We don't know how long that lasted, but a fruit and a snake got in the way. In shame, Adam and Eve hid from God. They didn't want anything to do with Him. Sin had entered the world, and with it, alienation from God. They were forced to leave God's paradise garden, the relationship ruined. They no longer wanted to walk with Him, but desired to go their own way (Genesis 1–3).

As time progressed, God became grieved by the people He had created. Their free will had become free sin. They disregarded Him and indulged in all sorts of perversions which His righteous nature could not tolerate. In His anger, He nearly destroyed everyone in a flood, except Noah and his family, who had found favor with God because of their righteousness (Genesis 6:5–8).

God is both a God of holiness and a God of love. Holiness requires judgement, but love dictates mercy. God promised to never again destroy the earth by a flood. Though Holy God still disciplined His people when they sinned, He was slow to anger and abounding in love (Psalm 86:15), not treating them as their sins deserved (Psalm 103:10). His discipline endeavored to bring them back into a relationship with Himself and help them be the best they could be. God loved His people so much that He continued to pursue this relationship, even though they continually disobeyed Him.

While they wandered in the desert after leaving Egypt, He dwelt in their midst in a visible pillar of cloud and fire. He took care of their needs, performing miracle after miracle: parting seas; providing water, manna and quail in the desert; giving them supernatural victories in battles; keeping their shoes and clothes from wearing out; protecting them; showering them with wealth and prosperity. He provided a way for His people to obtain His forgiveness for their sins through animal sacrifices, for His law decreed that there was no forgiveness of sin without the shedding of blood (Hebrews 9:22).

"In spite of all this [God's miracles], they kept on sinning, in spite of his wonders, they did not believe" (Psalm 78:32). Instead of loving God with all their hearts, souls and strength as God's law had commanded (Deuteronomy 6:5), they trembled with fear. They refused to talk to God directly, even though He was right there with them. They insisted on a human being delivering His message. They told Moses, "Speak to us yourself and we will listen. But do not have God speak to us or we will die" (Exodus 20:19). They even preferred lifeless idols to the Living God.

So, God talked to them through Moses, His laws and the prophets. The people would listen for a while, but soon reverted to their old ways. They broke the laws and their sacrifices were shams. They ridiculed the prophets. Ignoring God, they depended on their own abilities. Their rebellion brought numerous sorrows. Chapter 4 in the book of Amos tells the story of God pursuing His people, who had wandered far from Him and His love. He wanted them to turn their faces to Him, not their backs (Jeremiah 32:33), so He sent calamity after calamity. God used plagues, famine, drought, disasters, sickness—all kinds of trouble to try to get them to turn back to Him. But they were stiff-necked and hard hearted and still insisted on their own way.

> *Many times, he delivered them, but they were bent on rebellion and they wasted away in their sin. Yet he took note of their distress when he heard their cry; for their sake he remembered his covenant and out of his great love he relented.*
> (Psalm 106:43–45)

> *They refused to listen and failed to remember the miracles you performed among them.... But you are a forgiving God, gracious and compassionate, slow to anger and abounding in love. Therefore, you did not desert them....*
> (Nehemiah 9:17)

God knew that sin had enslaved them. They were caught in its powerful grip, helpless, bound as though by prison chains. They couldn't do what was right even if that had been their desire. God clearly demonstrated through them that laws were insufficient to establish righteousness and restore a relationship with Him (Romans 3:20), because they neither desired nor were able to follow them. In His immense love, He had a plan from the beginning to save them and set them free, rebuilding the relationship with Himself so that there could be reestablished communication. He would send the Messiah—Emmanuel, God with us.

We are in this same sin-grip, enslaved, unable and unwilling to follow God and His commands. We, too, are rebellious and turn from God even in our troubles, ignoring Him and going our own way, much to our detriment. Sin has alienated everyone from God and has prevented all of us from communicating with Him.

Yet our society has chosen to negate the idea of sin, thinking that "sin isn't bad. Believing in sin is."[14] Certain religions, especially Christianity, "insist that all people are bad and in need of saving, and that we all *have to* believe certain things about God, or face eternal consequences... [Our] approach should be more reasonable and humanistic in nature, with the emphasis on the ability of humans to be good"[15]

Unfortunately, this pervasive ideology—the humanistic belief that we are basically good and can therefore solve our own problems and don't need God—is erroneous and dangerous. That choice leads to our destruction, both now and eternally. We were created to be in relationship to God, but our sin nature prevents this. We become deluded, thinking God is not real, and if He is, He's irrelevant. We might even try to get to God our own way, but we fall short.

Romans 3:23 says that all have sinned and fallen short of the glory of God. "There is no one who always does what is right, not even one" (Romans 3:10 NCV). This verse from Isaiah describes the awfulness of sin: "We are all dirty with sin. Even our good works are not pure. They are like bloodstained rags. We are all like dead leaves. Our sins have carried us away like wind" (Isaiah 64:6 ERV). Sin has a way of elevating us and diminishing God, making us believe it is best to be self-sufficient and solve our own problems. But, we need Him. The story of the Hound of Heaven illustrated that as narrow as it may sound, the only way to satisfaction and a purposeful life is through turning to God. "Jesus answered, 'I am the way and the truth and the life. No one comes to the Father except through me'" (John 14:6). We can try other paths, but our lives will be meaningless and empty. God doesn't want to restrict us, but to bless us. He wants to communicate with us. Purporting the doctrine of Jesus as the one way is not being narrow-minded and intolerant, it's sharing the good news that there is a way out. There is salvation for all people—none is excluded.

In the beginning was the Word and the Word was with God, and the Word was God. The Word became flesh and made His dwelling among us (John 1:1, 14). This "Word" is Jesus, God's only Son, sent to earth as the Messiah-Savior, Emmanuel, God with us. Because of His incomparable love, Jesus came to rescue us from our sin-bondage and alienation from God. He didn't come as a mighty king or ruler to lord it over us and make us shape up (John 3:17), but as a sacrificial lamb, taking on Himself the sin-punishment we deserve by shedding His blood and dying on the cross. By His grace—unearned favor (Ephesians 2: 8–9)—He sets us free from laws we couldn't follow and from the penalty of our sins that leads to spiritual and eternal death. We are *declared righteous* in

God's eyes (Romans 3:21–24), not because of what we have done or do, but because of Jesus's cross work. "The underlying foundation of the Christian faith is [understanding the] undeserved, limitless miracle of the love of God that was exhibited on the Cross of Calvary; a love not earned and can never be."[16]

You see, at just the right time, when we were still powerless, Christ died for the ungodly. Very rarely will anyone die for a righteous person, though for a good person someone might possibly dare to die. But God demonstrates his own love for us in this: While we were still sinners, Christ died for us.
(Romans 5: 6–8)

God loves us more than we can imagine and pursues us, desiring a relationship with us like the one He enjoyed with Adam and Eve before sin ruined everything. "Jesus's death and resurrection was [God's] Master Plan to win back for man all that he had lost in Eden."[17] Jesus ends the enmity between people and God, removing the alienation caused by sin that started in the paradise-garden. We are reconciled to God—a friendship reestablished (Romans 5:10). We don't have to clean up our act first to come to God. He accepts us as we are. It is truly amazing that God sees all the twisted things about us, and more corruption in us than we see in ourselves, yet He still loves us and wants to be our friend![18] We were actually created to be in fellowship with God.

Jesus came to communicate God's words to us so that we could know God. Jesus is the light in darkness. Before we believe in Jesus, everything about Him is dark and confusing. Dallas Willard likens us to a kitten: biologically alive, but unable to understand mathematical concepts. That is what it means to be dead in sin—biologically alive, but dead to the things of God. His words are foolishness. We cannot understand His words any more than that kitten could understand math. We need an inward change, a rebirth, before we can hear God correctly.[19]

When we accept God's gift of grace by believing in Jesus, we come to life—reborn, a new creation (2 Corinthians 5:17). As we learn to know God, our reestablished relationship enables us to talk to Him as beloved children, and He will speak to us in an intimate way as our "Abba, Father" (translated as "Daddy") (Romans 8:15). We don't need a priest or advocate to go to God for us. We have the privilege of directly approaching "God's throne of grace with confidence, so that we may receive mercy and find grace to help us in our time of need" (Hebrews 4:16).

The result of this friendship is that God begins a work in our hearts and souls, helping us become the person He created us to be—free from the taint of sin that clouds our understanding and distorts His voice. He forgives our sins and heals all our diseases (Psalm 103:3), breaking the curse and making us whole. We don't need to fear that God will spoil our fun and make us give up everything that matters to us. We don't become dull, uninteresting people. God completes us, so that our natural, God-given abilities are maximized. His resurrection power is at work in us, transforming us, equipping us, and giving us all that we need to achieve an exciting, meaningful and abundant life in which we can communicate with Him as a friend.

His divine power has given us everything we need for a godly life through
our knowledge of him who called us by his own glory and goodness.
(2 Peter 1:3)

Yes, God wants us to be sanctified (holy), but the word doesn't mean thwarted, restricted and irrelevant. It means whole, fulfilled, happy and set apart for something special.[20] His Spirit changes our very desires and focus. Catherine Marshall wrote that "God will bring about such a change in us that His plans and desires for us will be our delight."[21]

Jeff's story illustrates how God can change our hearts to follow His will. Jeff was working at a prestigious job and felt God's call to leave and prepare for missions by going to Bible School. Here is his story.

"I met Emily. We hadn't even dated, but when I was driving home from school, God told me that she was going to be my wife and mother of my children. Before that moment, children were not something I wanted, but I had a sudden desire to have many children relatively quickly. Two days later, I asked Emily out on a date. In trepidation, I told her what God had told me. She shared my call and vision. We had only been dating two weeks and had known each other for only a month when I proposed. God gave us and everyone in our families complete peace about us getting married quickly. We were married two months later. God orchestrated all the details. I believe God speaks by placing complete peace in our hearts about a circumstance that we know from the Bible is within God's will. On the other hand, if He, through the Holy Spirit is trying to caution us, we will feel it on our hearts, too. What some may call a gut feeling may be God speaking."

So, where do you stand today? Do you want to ignore God and do things your own way? Do you fear His requirements and want to avoid Him? Do you have the best of intentions, but somehow haven't gotten around to forging a relationship with God? Is it too much trouble? Is the cost too great? Or, do you see the value and awesome privilege of accepting His love and grace, and turning to Him? You can have an intimate life-changing relationship with Almighty God who spoke the universe into being yet loves and cares about you! But you must make the choice.

On a cold November day, our youngest son Kurt and I headed to soccer practice. By the side of the road, high in a bare-branched tree, we saw something move. It was still there when we returned two hours later. We realized it was a kitten. We headed back to our house where Kurt got our ladder from the garage. Then we went back to the tree. Kurt climbed to the top of the ladder, but still couldn't reach the kitten, so he shimmied out on shaky branches, finally grasping her. She hissed and scratched him, apparently unaware that she was being rescued. We took her home and offered cat food and warm milk, but she hid under our couch on a beach towel for almost two days. Though we advertised, no one claimed her. Kurt was ready to love her and adopt her as his pet, but the kitten ignored him, unimpressed that he had rescued her. Instead, she chose our other son, Chris, and became his constant companion. Chris left shortly thereafter for college and the kitten was beside herself. She left our home, unable to form a bond with anyone else in the family.

Like Kurt's kitten, have we turned away from the one who loved and rescued us, choosing other uncertain affections that will let us down? Do we stubbornly refuse to change our minds? Jesus is waiting with open arms. Come.

The first step is personally accepting Jesus, God's gift of salvation by grace, by confessing our sins and believing in His death and resurrection (Romans 10:9). We then become friends with Him. Until we do, we are in darkness, unable to understand the things of God or hear His voice. When we step from our darkness into God's light, we are born into new life, becoming part of God's family. The Holy Spirit lives in us (John 14:16–17). The more we seek God, get to know Him and spend time with Him, the deeper our relationship with Him will become. It will become easier to hear Him, and we will be more aware of the fact that He hears us too. The result will be a life that is "exceedingly abundantly above all that we ask or think." (Ephesians 3: 20 NKJV) Oswald Chambers puts it this way: "The reason people are tired [dissatisfied] of life is that God has not given them anything—they have not been given their life 'as a prize.' (Jeremiah 45:5 NKJV). The way to get out of that condition is to abandon yourself to God. And once you do get to the point of total surrender to Him, you will be the most surprised and delighted person on earth."[22]

I want you to know, my very dear friends, that it is on account of this resurrected Jesus that the forgiveness of your sins can be promised. He accomplishes, in those who believe, everything that the Law of Moses could never make good on. But everyone who believes in this raised-up Jesus is declared good and right and whole before God.
(Acts 13:38 MSG)

Entering into a relationship with Jesus is the first step to communicating with Him. Then, what an adventure awaits! My computer screen saver shows various pictures with teaser captions. One caption read, "The adventure begins." And so it does.

"And what adventure God's speaking directly to us brings to life!"[23]

—◆ *Stop and Refresh* ◆—

1. Read Joshua 24: 15–27. What does this tell you about God? God is a God of both holiness and love. He is a jealous God. Do these characteristics conflict with your idea of God? Do you see evidence of these aspects of God today? How does this apply to your relationship with Him?

2. If we are supposed to be in a relationship with God, why do you think it is so difficult?

3. Sin has a way of elevating us and diminishing God. What do you think this means? How do you see this at work in our society?

4. Read Romans 3:9–24. What does it mean to be "declared righteous" and transformed? How does this happen and what is the result? What is meant by "God completes us?

5. Do you believe there is only one way to God? Explain. What scriptures support your opinion? What do you have to do to establish a relationship with God? What has God done to make this possible?

Chapter Four

ROAD TRIP

Where do we go to find God?

The Lord says, "Let my people return to me. Remove every obstacle from their path! Build the road and make it ready!"
(Isaiah 57:14 GNT)

B y now you should be convinced, or at least be entertaining the idea, that God desires a relationship with you and wants to talk with you. He loves you. He made you to be unique and significant. Once you accept His grace and love by believing in Him, you become part of His family and enter the amazing relationship where you have access to God and His promises. What can be more thrilling and satisfying than having the God who spoke the universe into being by His words, communicate with you? Yes, *you*. Do you want to begin the journey to a closer relationship with God so He can speak to you?

When taking a trip, one must first decide where to go, then prepare. Months before my husband and I go on a road trip, we pick a destination. We assess the cost and time necessary. We make sure our car is clean and in good working order. I plan. I research where we are going to make sure we see all the highlights and get the best values. Yelp, Fodor's and AAA have helpful reviews on dining, sightseeing and lodging. I get a map and plan the route, checking with Map Quest for driving times. When all the data is in, I make a detailed itinerary with phone and confirmation numbers, and a schedule. We fill the car with gas, pack some snacks and are on our way.

Choosing the Destination

As with our road trip, the first step in journeying to a relationship with God is determining the destination. Do we want to enter a relationship with God and communicate with Him? Do we want an intimate, paradise-garden type of relationship, or are we satisfied with mediocre spirituality? Do we talk big, but act small, going halfway and cutting corners?[24]

Many have a relationship with God in which they check with Him only when absolutely necessary. "We regard God as an airman regards his parachute; it's there for emergencies, but he hopes he'll never have to use it."[25] We treat God this way, then wonder why our spiritual lives are so unsatisfying, our prayers aren't answered, and we don't hear God.

There are people who don't like to take road trips. They prefer to stay home and relax, avoiding the stress and cost of traveling. If they do go somewhere, they don't plan and just go with the flow, enjoying whatever comes their way. While this may work for vacations, it isn't an advisable method for a journey towards God. Oswald Chambers notes that "many of us prefer to stay at the entrance to the Christian life, instead of going on to create and build our souls in accordance with the new life God has placed within us."[26] Moving toward a closer relationship with God, doesn't just happen. It takes concentrated intentionality. Do you want to move forward? Do you want something more? The old hymn, *In the Garden*, by Charles Miles, describes the paradise-garden relationship that we can develop with God.

> *I come to the garden alone,*
> *While the dew is still on the roses,*
> *And the voice I hear, falling on my ear*

The Son of God discloses.
And He walks with me,
And He talks with me,
And He tells me I am His own;
And the joy we share as we tarry there,
None other has ever known.27

To communicate with God on a deeper level, we must seek an enduring quality relationship with Him, submitting to His way, dwelling in His presence, and putting in the time necessary to develop that relationship. When Perry and I became engaged, we never wanted to be apart, because of our deep love for one another. We ate meals together, we attended classes together, we studied together. Every day we enjoyed each other's company as much as we could. This developed a close interpersonal relationship in which we came to know each other well.

As our love for God grows and we understand His love for us, we will desire to be with Him and do things for Him. "The individual that is closer to God receives clearer communication....We should look forward to the time when our interaction with God is quiet and constant for our guidance and usefulness in ministry as we do the work God has placed before us."[28] When we focus on God and His work, joining Him in what He is doing, instead of running about attending to our own business, we are creating a storehouse of eternal treasures that will last, not stockpiling perishable earthly accomplishments for our own glory (Matthew 6:19–22).

Jesus never gives us the choice to join Him halfway. We shouldn't accept Christianity merely for "fire insurance," figuring we can live however we please by relying on God's grace to save us in the end (Romans 6:1). Dietrich Bonhoeffer calls this cheap grace—grace without a cost, without repentance, without discipleship.[29] James questions the reality of our faith if we aren't acting on it (James 2). "We can't stroll into Christlikeness with our hands in our pockets"[30] "God's grace produces men and women with a strong family likeness to Jesus Christ, not pampered, spoiled weaklings."[31]

We should be maturing, growing, and aligning ourselves more closely to God, but we should not make the mistake of letting Christian disciplines lead to our own self-realization and holiness, focusing on our own good works. This ultimately brings glory to ourselves and our service, not Jesus.[32] As we conform to His image, we are minimized, and He is maximized.

If your first concern is to look after yourself, you'll never find yourself. But if you forget about yourself and look to Me, you'll find both yourself and Me.
(Matthew 10:39, MSG)

Considering the Cost

"Luther had said that grace alone can save; his followers took up his doctrine and repeated it word for word. But they left out its invariable corollary, the obligation to discipleship ... The justification of the sinner in the world degenerated into the justification of sin and the world. Costly grace was turned into cheap grace without discipleship."[33]

While grace alone can save, we must remember that we should not go on sinning so that grace may increase. (Romans 6:1) We are free from sin, but become slaves to righteousness, having an obligation to follow Jesus's directives. When we focus merely on love and grace, we miss the discipleship component. Is traveling to the destination of a relationship with God worth this kind of time and effort? Let's consider the cost—the investment needed.

Suppose one of you wants to build a tower. Won't you first sit down and estimate the cost to see if you have enough money to complete it?
(Luke 14:28)

If we truly want to hear God and walk in a paradise-garden type of relationship with Him, it will cost. Everything. We lose what we know of our lives to find new lives (Matthew 16:25). We'll relinquish our wills. We'll submit to Him and obey His precepts. We must deny ourselves, take up our crosses and follow Him, regardless of what the world says (Matthew 16:24). "To deny oneself is to be aware only of Christ and no more of self..."[34] This is a radical readjustment.

Everything else in our lives—our relationships, our possessions and our plans—become secondary to following Jesus. "Anyone who loves their father or mother more than me is not worthy of me; anyone who loves their son or daughter more than me is not worthy of me" (Matthew 10:37).

I learned this principle the hard way. My husband Perry and I were attending the Fort Benning main post chapel in Georgia. Chaplain Landers, the tall, black Baptist preacher entered along with his coworker, Chaplain Stuart, a small bespectacled white Episcopalian priest. In military chapels, all protestant denominations are merged under one roof. The service began with the robed chancel choir entering to an organ prelude and a stately hymn, while acolytes, dressed in their white robes, lit the altar candles. Then, the gospel choir entered, singing loudly, clapping hands and swaying to a jazzy spiritual. Usually, I was quite amused at this unlikely blend that somehow worked to erase the lines of denominations and culture, but today, my heart was heavy.

Days before, our pediatrician had diagnosed our baby daughter with cystic fibrosis. She was due to enter the children's hospital in Atlanta for a week of tests. She had not been growing and developing according to their charts and at almost a year, was only twelve pounds, didn't crawl and showed no signs of standing. The sweat chloride test for CF, administered because of her "failure to thrive," had come back positive.

I felt distant from the praise and worship surrounding me. Even Chaplain Landers' "Do I hear an Amen?" failed to rouse me. I was having a silent struggle with God. How could He allow my precious baby to be less than perfect? How could He allow this harm to come to me? Where was He in my hour of need? I was angry at Him and demanded His intervention.

Chaplain Landers' booming sermon was on Abraham and Isaac (Genesis 22). He told the story with flair, and the congregation cheered him on. He said that God will do what God will do. He doesn't have to have our permission. What He does want is our unwavering trust and our unfaltering obedience. We must be willing to give up anything that would stand in the way of our relationship to Him.

I imagined how difficult it must have been for Abraham to offer up his special son, given to him and Sarah in their old age. Yet he obeyed and trusted God, without question. Somehow Abraham had faith that God was a good God and that His purposes were just.

God spoke to me in that moment—not in an audible voice that those around me could hear, but in a powerful voice that ripped into my soul. Who was I to take possession of this life God had given me? My daughter really belonged to him. I felt like Abraham as I tearfully offered her to Him and said that I allowed Him to do with her as He pleased, trusting that He ultimately is good and loves both me and her. At that moment, a peace came over me. I no longer feared what might happen. I knew that if I must walk this road, God would be with me. I let go. She was His.

The week in the hospital was indeed an ordeal. I became very agitated at the incessant poking and prodding that woke her (and me) at night and caused her to cry a lot. The spinal tap was especially difficult. Finally, she was released. The whole staff of doctors were clueless. They could find nothing wrong, but nothing had changed. I left the hospital with an arsenal of medications and regimens. They told me that she would always be small and nonathletic, spending her time reading and being involved with inactive projects.

We moved shortly thereafter to Illinois. Since we were not near a military base, we were assigned a local pediatrician, who turned out to be a no-nonsense woman in her sixties, who had been practicing medicine for forty years. She sat me down and said with authority, "Look, there is nothing wrong with your daughter. It doesn't matter whether or not she measures up to their graphs and charts. She is perfectly healthy and will do what she wants to do in her own way and at her own pace." This was liberating and dispelled my concern.

As we look back on this time, we now chuckle. Our daughter is taller than I am. She became an accomplished soccer player, making the Midwest Regional Olympic Development Team, playing varsity soccer in high school and getting a college scholarship. So much for the predictions.

I don't know if God actually healed her from cystic fibrosis or another disease. What I do know is that He spoke to me in no uncertain terms back in that military chapel, telling me to get my priorities straight. All that I am, and all that I have are His. I've been given the duty and privilege of being the caretaker of my children, my husband, my house, my possessions and my life. God can choose to take any of these things at any time. Our God is a jealous God who wants nothing to get in the way of our relationship with Him. Yet, like Abraham, we must trust in His love and goodness even when we don't understand what He's doing.

God provided a ram for Abraham so he didn't have to sacrifice His son. When we trust God implicitly, He provides for us too. Catherine Marshall made me smile when I read her devotion that said, "God is always working on the 'ram part'—the escape."[35] When we put these two words together—rampart—we see an image of His strong protection that surrounds us and supports us throughout every challenge. We can rest in the assurance that it's not up to us. He's got it covered.

Fred also learned that God must come first. He loved his car—a shiny, black Opal GT that he considered to be the "poor man's Corvette." When he drove it, wearing his stylish leather jacket, he felt "cool." On his way home from work, the car started to shake. He pulled into a service station and they repaired what they assessed to be the problem. A few miles down the road, the problem reoccurred— another service station, another repair, another bill. He was prompted to pray, "Lord, if you want me to get rid of this car, I will." Next, he pulled onto a Chicago toll road. This time the car stopped. Dead. Right in the middle of the toll road. He couldn't get over, and there were no service stations. It was rush hour and dark. Though he put on his flashers, a black SUV hit him hard from behind. Miraculously, he was okay, though his car was totaled. Fred believes this was God's way of telling him to get rid of that car, because it had become too important to him. He was thankful for God's unbelievable protection in the accident.

The cost of discipleship is tremendous. We must let nothing come between us and God, for He is a jealous God, demanding our all. Anything that absorbs our focus or steals our affections—possessions, people, and plans—are idols. We must relinquish everything to His control. We are warned about remaining "lukewarm" in our faith—a blasé apathy to God's directives. In Revelation 3, God addresses the church in Laodicea. They think they have it all together. They think they are rich and need nothing. Yet God condemns them as "lukewarm" and says He will "spit them out of His mouth" (Revelation 3:16).

> *But since you are like lukewarm water, neither hot nor cold,*
> *I will spit you out of my mouth! … I correct and discipline*
> *everyone I love. So be diligent and turn from your indifference.*
> (Revelation 3:16–19 NLT)

We know that to keep our bodies healthy, we must make healthy choices and stick to them. It's the same with healthy spirits. We must decide that pursuing God with discipline is a non-negotiable spiritual habit we are determined to develop.[36] However, the idea of totally submitting and denying ourselves may seem very uninviting. What happened to grace? What happened to unearned favor from God? We can't possibly follow what is required of us. You may be thinking, "I'm not skilled enough. I'm not disciplined enough. I'm afraid of what God will ask me to do." The sheer magnitude of this causes us to back off lest we succumb to what Bill Hybels calls a "straightjacket experience filled with requirements that squeeze the vitality and spontaneity, and adventure right out of faith and life."[37]

It is not God's intent to burden us, but to free us. He doesn't want us to consider a relationship with Him as one of impossible demands, duty and diligence. He wants us to place our burdens on Him and rest in Him, being refreshed and renewed as we dwell in His presence. (Matthew 11:28–29). He wants us to depend on Him, trust Him and not worry. Our relationship with God is not about our efforts to be holy, but submitting to His transforming work in us that turns us into the accomplished, complete person He created us to be. There is no pain in ceasing to do what we no longer care to do.[38] "[Our] part is to yield to [His] creative work in [us], neither resisting it nor trying to speed it up."[39] God is the ultimate artist. He who paints sunsets, builds mountains, and sculpts flowers can make each of us into something beautiful. Relax and enjoy Him.

He who began a good work in you will carry it
on to completion until the day of Christ Jesus."
(Philippians 1:6)

Our pastor, Nate Powell, spoke about developing a deeper relationship with God. He called it "giving God an all-access passkey." When Nate has rented condos on vacation, the key he is given opens the door only to the rooms his family is allowed to use. They can't move or change anything. However, if he owned the condo, he could use it all. The key would have full access. As the owner, he would have the right to change, update or to move things around. Are we willing to give God ownership? Can He have the full-access passkey to our lives? Can He change us? Or, have we only given Him access to certain rooms of our lives, allowing no changes and keeping places to ourselves? Being a disciple of Jesus means giving our all.

Ryan made a tough choice to follow Jesus. His passion was football. Would he be willing to lay this aside and pursue Christian ministry? Here is his story.

Ryan grew up in a Christian home, attending church regularly. He accepted Jesus at an early age, but figures he made the decision because those who did got to go to a party and get a cupcake. He liked cupcakes.

His life didn't change very much. He didn't understand what it meant to be in a committed relationship with Jesus. He thought that as long as he was a good, moral person and stayed out of trouble, he would be saved.

When Ryan was in high school, his life began to change. He avoided youth group and church. His passion was football, and it began to consume his life. He played football, he practiced football, he trained for football, and he thought about football all the time. His heart was drawn away from God as he was drawn away from the church.

In the summer between his sophomore and junior years of high school, for some reason, he signed up to go on a church mission trip to Romania. On this trip, his heart came alive as he helped serve people as the hands and feet of Jesus. He had joy inside, developing a passion for serving others. He was beginning to understand what it meant to be a Christian—to love God and love others.

At the end of the trip, God confronted him with John 6:66–68. In this passage, Jesus had hundreds of followers, but as his teaching became more controversial and difficult, many left. Jesus asked Peter, "Are you going to leave too?" Ryan felt like Jesus was asking him this same question. Ryan had to make a choice. When he got back home, would he go on living the same way, or was he going to make the change and follow Jesus? His heart's response was the same as Peter's. "Lord, to whom shall I go? You have the words of eternal life."

Back at home, Ryan still played football, trying to juggle it with his new responsibilities as a Christ-follower: loving God and loving others. After some hard discussions and prayerful moments, he realized that if he was going to be serious about fully following Jesus, he would have to quit football, because it was consuming him. People thought he was crazy to quit. His coach told him that if he quit football, he would quit everything else in his life. Others didn't understand the singleness of purpose, and the importance of giving up everything to follow Jesus. The cost was great, but the rewards were far greater. Now, sixteen years later, Ryan is passionately serving the Lord as a youth pastor, a calling he believes is from the Lord. Does Ryan still love football? Of course he does, but God has trumped this affection with another higher passion. Serving God and serving others is the foremost desire of his heart.

Seriously pursuing God requires adjustments to the way we do things, a new focus, a change of heart and revamped priorities. God is willing to make that transformation in us by changing our very desires, if we will allow Him to do so. "…we'll be surprised to find that where we once resisted His direction as being too difficult or risky or potentially embarrassing, we now find we want it—at least more than we want the alternative of moving forward without Him."[40] But He doesn't force Himself on us. He waits patiently for us to relinquish our wills to Him and give Him the reins. We don't have to struggle, working hard, being frustrated and feeling like we are getting nowhere in the pursuit of holiness. We need to let go and let God do the work in us. It doesn't happen all at once. It's a process of becoming. It's work. It's commitment. Sometimes, it's painful and difficult. It's worth it.

"[Discipleship] is costly because it costs a man his life, and it is grace because it gives a man the only true life."[41]

I will give them a heart to know me, that I am the Lord. They will be my people, and I will be their God, for they will return to me with all their heart.
(Jeremiah 24:7)

——◆ *Stop and Refresh* ◆——

1. Read Genesis 3. What is meant by the term "paradise-garden" relationship? How was the relationship ruined? Do you think it is possible to restore this relationship? Why or why not?

2. We are told to "deny ourselves, take up our cross and follow Jesus." What does this involve? Is it possible to follow Jesus without doing this? Is making this commitment practical for us today?

3. Read Luke 14:26–33. What does it mean to "hate your father, mother, wife, children, brothers and sisters"?

4. Compare Exodus 34:14, Galatians 5: 19–21 and 2 Corinthians 11:2. Jealousy is considered a sin, yet God is described as a jealous God. How do you explain this?

5. The Bible says we are saved by faith, not works. Discipleship seems to involve a great deal of work, that seems impossible to do right. How do you resolve this? (Read Ephesians 2:8–9, James 2: 14–17 and Philippians 1:6.)

Chapter Five

GET GOING

Open the doors and move out.

*Therefore let us move beyond the elementary teachings
about Christ and be taken forward to maturity.*
(Hebrews 6:1)

The next step in moving toward an intimate relationship with God is clearing the way. When our car is parked in the garage, we won't get very far on our road trip if we keep the door closed. It appears safe and secure in that dark room, but we are prevented from traveling.

What gets in the way of our journey toward God? Though God may choose to break through the barriers we have constructed and talk to us, developing continual, effective communication with God requires a clear, open channel. We must open the door.

*Look! I stand at the door and knock. If you hear my voice and open
the door, I will come in, and we will share a meal together as friends.*
(Revelation 3:20 NLT)

In order to open the doors of our hearts and minds to God's interaction with us, we need to pay attention to God's directives in His Word, the Bible. He provides the key to hearing His voice. "He will be the sure foundation for your times, a rich store of salvation and wisdom and knowledge; the fear of the LORD is the key to this treasure" (Isaiah 33:6).

I love to snorkel. When we visited Molokini Crater off the coast of Maui, I was enthralled by the colorful sea life visible in the clear water. Caught up in my own undersea world, my ears were plugged, and I couldn't hear the signal to return to our tour boat. Someone had to tap me on the shoulder to get my attention. I was disappointed that it was time to leave.

> *Their ears are closed so they cannot hear. The word of the*
> *Lord is offensive to them; they find no pleasure in it.*
> (Jeremiah 6:10)

Sin plugs our ears and hardens our hearts, building a wall between us and God. God is always there, ready for us to seek Him, but we get caught up in our own affairs, and don't pay attention. Even inconspicuous sins of neglect and self-centeredness obstruct our relationship to God. He doesn't turn away from us. He keeps tapping us on the shoulder. We are the ones that construct the barriers and clog the system so our vehicle can't move close enough to Him to hear Him.

A little girl illustrated this principle well. While sitting in church with her parents, Karen drew pictures. Her parents had told her to draw something she heard in either the songs or the pastor's message. She drew several rectangles stacked on top of one another. In the next picture, the rectangles were strewn all over the page, and a large hand was reaching down from the top of the paper. After the service, while the family ate lunch, they asked Karen to explain her pictures.

The rectangles depicted bricks, which represented sins. Sin-bricks stack up making a wall between us and God. The more bricks, or sins, in the wall, the more we are blocked from God. But, God reaches down, forgiving sin and knocking down the wall. We have access to God again.

This perceptive little girl understood a principle that many of us have not yet grasped. If we want to see and hear God, we need to get the blockage of sin out of the way so that we can see and hear Him more effectively. We can't do this by ourselves, but we have incredible help. God reaches down to us, even in our sin, to save us and forgive us, knocking away those sin-bricks. No sin poses too great of a challenge for God, nor is any sin too insignificant for His attention.

> *But your iniquities have separated you from your God; your*
> *sins have hidden his face from you, so that he will not hear.*
> (Isaiah 59: 2)

> *When we were overwhelmed by sins, you forgave our transgressions.*
> (Psalm 65: 3)

Let God break down the wall that stands between you and Him by confessing your sin and accepting His forgivingness. When we confess our sins, it's not for God, it's for us. Jesus has already forgiven all our sins—once for all—by His death on the cross (Hebrews 7:27). But our sin compels us to turn from God and hide from Him, just like Adam and Eve hid from God in the garden. Our dark hiding places seem safe and secure from God's requirements, but they are not. They're restrictive, imprisoning us so we can't move and can't hear. Confession brings us back into God's light where He can forgive, cleanse, restore and heal us.[42] Let His forgiveness unstop your ears and open your heart to His words for you, so you're not hindered. He has promised:

> *If we confess our sins, he is faithful and just and will*
> *forgive us our sins and purify us from all unrighteousness.*
> (1 John 1: 9)

In the presence of God, we examine our hearts and let Him show us specific sins that need our attention and His forgiveness. When we do confess our sins, we don't lay our overall sinful state before God and say, "Wipe it all clean," though God does do that. This attitude can be both a cop out—a failure to spend time truly examining ourselves so that we can change by God's power—or a dump down where we are overwhelmed by the magnitude of our sins and feel totally inadequate. God will show us one area at a time and help us address it as we turn it over to Him, His power will enable us to be victorious over it.

Preparing our Vehicle

Before my husband and I go on a trip, we do several things to get our car ready. We like to have our car power-washed. Our local station does a great job of making the outside clean and shiny, but more importantly, they vacuum and wipe down the interior, making it spotless. They even add a pleasant fragrance. This makes traveling so much more enjoyable.

I was amused when my friend Jim told me he uses his shower for more than body cleansing. As he confesses his sins, he envisions God washing away the guilt of his iniquities while the water washes the dirt from his body, sending it all forever down the drain.

God's forgiving power cleanses us too, from the inside out, getting rid of all the unpleasant dirt and grime. He makes us to be a sweet aroma of His presence.

Wash away all my iniquity and cleanse me from my sin.
(Psalm 51:2)

But I thank God, who always leads us in victory because of Christ. Wherever we go, God uses us to make clear what it means to know Christ. It's like a fragrance that fills the air.
(2 Corinthians 2:14 GW)

Ruth also shared a story about God using her shower to wash away the things that were keeping her from an open relationship to Him. In her case, she was dealing with feelings of anger, shock, betrayal, and unforgiveness after her husband of over thirty-three years abruptly left their marriage. Here is her story:

"It was a slow but steady process of His tender hands restoring my very crushed heart. But He did it. I was giving a birthday party for our daughter who was visiting from England. This would be the third time I had encountered my ex-husband since the divorce, and I was nervous.

A couple of days before the party, I was in the shower. Suddenly, I heard very clearly in my mind, "You can forgive him now." I immediately felt a sense of relief. I wept as I sensed that the shower water was God's presence pouring over me, washing away the bitterness, anger and hurt. My Father's words were not ones of condemnation and impatience—'get on with it Ruth, it's been long enough.' He knew my heart was ready now and He restored and rebuilt my heart so that I could forgive."

Our horizonal relationships affect our vertical one. Mark 11:24–25 tells us that we must first forgive others so that we can be forgiven. First Peter 3:7 underscores the importance of good marriage relationships, lest our prayers be hindered.[43] Unforgiveness, bitterness and a heart set on revenge not only block God's interaction with us but can compromise our physical well-being. Unforgiveness interrupts our fellowship with God. Do we want to hold a grudge, or have our prayers answered?[44]

In her book, *Moments That Matter*, Catherine Marshall told a story of a friend who had been wronged by her husband. She was bent on revenge and her health began to suffer. When she asked for advice, she was told that bitterness is destructive. She should try returning good for evil as Jesus commanded (Matthew 5:43–48). With Jesus's help, she managed to exhibit love and kindness to her husband. Good health returned, and her marriage prospered.[45]

A neighbor of mine was grouchy. Her husband, a military officer, was gone all the time, leaving her to manage her three kids alone. We lived on the post in Hawaii, and she missed her family on the mainland. On top of that, she resented me for having friends and always embarking on fun excursions. Though I tried to include her, she reneged. We were too religious for her. In her bitterness, she started attacking me by spreading rumors and doing unkind things to me and my kids.

I mostly ignored her, but God spoke to me and told me to return good for her evil. I began praying for ways to show kindness to her. She had minor surgery, and though her husband took the day off, he was soon back to his rigorous schedule. I offered to help her and bring her meals. In desperation, she grudgingly accepted. With my kindness, her attacks subsided, but she never thanked me. About a year later, they received orders to move. She called me and asked me to come over. "I don't understand why you were so nice to me when I was so hateful to you," she said. I was able to share the love of Jesus with her. "Love is not rude, is not selfish, and does not get upset with others. Love does not count up wrongs that have been done" (1 Corinthians 13:5 NCV).

We prepare to hear and see God by becoming clean and pure, getting rid of the bad attitudes even when we feel they're justified. It is the pure in heart who will see [and hear] God (Matthew 5:8). He washes out our minds, and in place of confusion, falsehood, hatred, anger, bitterness, suspicion and fear, He brings clarity, truth, love, forgiveness, confidence and hopefulness, developing the character in us which helps us hear Him clearly. God will do the purifying, if we allow it. He washes away the negative attitudes. He will open the channels in our spirit so that we have clear access to Him, and He has unobstructed access to us.

Create in me a pure heart, O God, and renew a steadfast spirit within me.
(Psalm 51:10)

As I have learned more about what pleases and displeases God, I have developed a broader understanding of sin. It's not just breaking a law like cheating, stealing or lying. It is not just harboring ungodly attitudes like bitterness and unforgiveness. It is more. I have discovered sin can be any malfunction in our heart attitude: self-sufficiency, arrogance, doubt or rebellion. Ignoring what God tells us to do is sin. Criticism, gossip and ungratefulness also displease God. Judging and showing favoritism doesn't conform to His will. In fact, James describes sin as knowing the good we ought to do and not doing it (James 4:17). When we come to God for His forgiveness, we learn an amazing truth about Him: not only does He forgive us, remembering our sins no more (Isaiah 43:25), but He also loves us, uses us, and speaks to us even as flawed vehicles. Don't feel you aren't of value to God if He's still working on you. God's transforming work in our lives is a continual process that will never be completed until we reach heaven.

The Holy Spirit will convict us of sin and lead us into the light of God's truth, but He doesn't ask us to clean up our act by ourselves. He asks for our acceptance of the truth about what in us needs fixing, and then He will make it right, by changing our very desires—changing us from the inside out.

The Holy Spirit doesn't condemn. "Therefore, there is now no condemnation for those who are in Christ Jesus" (Romans 8:1). If we're feeling guilty, condemned, unworthy and worthless—this is not of God. Satan is trying to steal our joy, and keep us in bondage to our sin, denying God's forgiving power. Don't let Satan fool you and keep you down. God wants you to soar on wings like an eagle, to run and not be weary, to walk and not faint. Wait on Him for His renewing power. (Isaiah 40:31) He forgives sin. He fixes the brokenness. He sets captives free. He restores life.

Restore to me the joy of your salvation and
grant me a willing spirit, to sustain me.
(Psalm 51:12)

Necessary Maintenance

A car has lots of parts that need to be in good working order before successfully going on a road trip. We don't want to break down. We may need to take our car to a mechanic for maintenance. We all need spiritual tune-ups too. When we place our lives in God's hands and depend on Him, He makes the necessary adjustments to help our vehicle "run smoother."

Regular car maintenance usually includes oil and oil filter changes. Dirty oil and filters cause extra wear and tear on our car's engine. Our spirit may also need a change. Are there thoughts that sully our system, clogging it so that focusing on God is difficult? The Bible cautions us to think on things that are true, honest, just, pure, lovely, of good report, virtuous and praiseworthy (Philippians 4:8). These are the things that mobilize us. We need to filter out negative, impure and destructive thoughts that tarry.

What we put into our car also makes a difference. If our car requires diesel or high-octane gas, we can't use regular. To see and hear God clearly, we also need to fill our spirit with God's spirit, not the opinions and practices of the world. How easily we can be sucked into media messages which distort truth and fill our minds with ungodly images. "Do not conform to the pattern of this world, but be transformed by the renewing of your mind" (Romans 12:2).

A car won't go very far with a flat tire. The indicator light on our dash tells us when our tire pressure needs adjusting, so we stop and add air, careful to follow the recommended PSI (pounds per square inch). Then we can keep going confidently. Depression, unworthiness and fear can make our spirits feel flat and unable to do very much or go very far. Put "air in your tires" with the invigorating breath of the Spirit. He will restore our spirit with the understanding of God's unconditional love and acceptance, for God does not show favoritism (Romans 2:10).

The Spirit regulates us to just the right pressure, too. If our air is too low, we feel sluggish and defeated. If we are too full, just like our car tires, we can have a blowout. Many of us have the tendency to take on too many obligations, causing a spiritual blowout. Pay attention to your PSI (prompting of the Spirit internally). We should let God's love, acceptance and grace fill us. God's perfect love drives out fear (1 John 4:18) and reminds us that we matter to Him. We don't need an over-abundance of activities to validate ourselves or impress Him. He accepts us just as we are, wanting us to rest in Him.

Most of us have experienced the r-r-r-r of a dead battery. Our car won't start until the battery is charged. My son-in-law drives a Tesla and knows where all the charging stations are so he can keep it running by plugging it in. Some stations "supercharge" completing the power transfer in about fifteen minutes. Our spiritual batteries need charging too. Doubt saps our power and paralyzes our faith and trust, stopping us dead in our tracks. We lose sight of God and struggle to do everything on our own. James 1:6–7 tells us that when we doubt we won't receive anything from the Lord. Let's recharge our batteries by plugging in to God's Word and promises. A time set aside for God is our supercharge.

Even with a charged battery, our car engines might not run because of faulty spark plugs. They may need to be changed as part of our maintenance. When our power levels are low because troubles sap our energy, remembering God's great deeds and promises, and praising Him, are surefire sparks to ignite our faith. Praise lifts us above our own issues, and thankfulness puts our focus on God and His power instead of the storms of life. Peter walked on water as long as he looked at Jesus, but he began to sink when he noticed the wind (Matthew 14:30). We must keep trusting Jesus through the storm even when we don't see the answer. He is the spark that gives us life and power.

Distractions and busyness can keep us from God too. Does our timing need an adjustment? In our car, a timing belt synchronizes the rotation of the crankshaft and the camshaft(s) so that the engine's valves open and close at the proper times. When the timing belt in our car runs too fast or slow, it causes engine problems. We need to remain in sync with God too—being ready when He calls us, and waiting for Him instead of running ahead on our own. Sometimes our "battle is not against sin, difficulties or circumstances, but against being so absorbed in our service to Jesus Christ that we are not ready to face Jesus Himself...." Without God, our plans break. "Depend on the Lord in whatever you do. Then your plans will succeed" (Proverbs 16:3 ICB). True success is impossible without God, for without God we can do nothing (John 15:5).

We're ready. Let's open the door and move out. Be washed inside and out, developing the sweet fragrance of Jesus. Head to the ultimate mechanic for maintenance and be in good working order. Let's fill up with God's spirit. The most incredible journey awaits. We're on our way to intimate communication with God.

As we proceed and travel the road of life, we won't know what's ahead. We must trust God and "walk by faith and not by sight" (2 Corinthians 5:7 NKJV). God will constantly be working on us to make sure we can navigate whatever comes. If we encounter road blocks, speed bumps and pot holes, He'll be there to help. We can be confident, though, that He has great things in store for us. Let's go!

How abundant are the good things that you have
stored up for those who fear you, that you bestow in
the sight of all, on those who take refuge in you.
(Psalm 31:19)

I will go before you and will level the mountains; I will break down
gates of bronze and cut through bars of iron. I will give you hidden
treasures, riches stored in secret places, so that you may know that I
am the LORD, the God of Israel, who summons you by name.
(Isaiah 45:2–3)

─────•◦ *Stop and Refresh* ◦•─────

1. Read James 4:17. Define sin. What other Bible passages talk about sin? Read Proverbs 6:16–19 and Galatians 5:19–20. Do these passages list things that we usually consider to be sins? In God's eyes is there a hierarchy of sin—some worse than others?

2. How do we get rid of sin and become pure in God's sight? Is this something we do, or something God does, or both?

3. God's forgiveness of us and our forgiveness of others are important steps in developing our relationship to God. Why must we not hold grudges against other people? Look up some verses on forgiveness and discuss them. Here's a start: Psalm 32:1, Psalm 130:4, Jeremiah 31:34, Matthew 6:12–15, Ephesians 1:7, Colossians 3:13, 1 John 1:9. You may find others.

4. Read Luke 6: 27–36. Is there a person in your life whom you find hard to forgive? Do you have a justifiable grudge? How does God want you to act toward that person? What can you do to return good for evil?

5. What are some things that obstruct our relationship to God? Discuss how we can fix this.

Chapter Six

STOP FOR DIRECTIONS
The Bible is our guidebook.

For the word of the Lord is right and true; he is faithful in all he does.
(Psalm 33:4)

I've always wanted to see the Canadian Rockies, so a group of us planned a road trip to Jasper and Banff National Parks. As I looked at our route on the map, I noticed we would go very close to an area where wild horses roamed. Friends told us that seeing them would be an unforgettable experience. Online maps showed places where herds typically congregate, and tours were not too expensive, so we planned to view the horses as our first stop. When I read more, however, I found out that the visitor's center closed in early afternoon and was not open on weekends. Also, tours had to be scheduled in advance. We had to adjust our schedule to align with this new data. Otherwise, we would have been disappointed. We were grateful we were prepared with the right information.

When planning a trip, I learn about my destination by researching it. Then I know what to see, where to look and have the needed information for successful sightseeing. We also prepare for our journey to intimacy with God by getting to know Him better through reading His Word, the Bible. When we don't know God, we don't recognize His voice, and may miss what He wants to show and tell us.

> *Be diligent to present yourself approved to God, a worker who*
> *does not need to be ashamed, rightly dividing the word of truth.*
> (2 Timothy 2:15 NKJV)

The primary way that God speaks to us and teaches us about Himself is through His Word, so if we want to hear from God, we need to delve into it. Charles Schultz drew a cartoon that shows a young man holding a Bible, while talking to a friend on the phone. The caption reads, "I think I've made one of the first steps toward unraveling the mysteries of the Old Testament…I'm starting to read it."[46] "A commitment to read and follow God's Word begins a daily journey of discovering God's love and power."[47] George Müller discovered the importance of "Soul Nourishment" through Scripture reading. He wrote:

"How different, when the soul is refreshed and made happy early in the morning, from what it is when without spiritual preparation, the service, the trials, and the temptations of the day come upon one. It has pleased the Lord to teach me a truth. I saw more clearly than ever that the first great and primary business to which I ought to attend every day was, to have my soul happy in the Lord. The first thing to be concerned about was not how much I might serve the Lord, or how I might glorify the Lord; but how my inner man might be nourished."[48]

Mr. Müller went on to note that all our endeavors in service, evangelism and personal godliness are ineffective unless we are nourished and strengthened in our inner beings day by day by reading God's Word.

A quick injection of knowledge from a Sunday sermon or short devotions isn't enough. While those are valuable, they don't provide the depth needed for an intimate, personal relationship with God. Though He often speaks to us through these means, we must be careful. We are receiving God's Word second-hand, a hand-me-down that may have flaws. Devotion books entertain, but they might distort verses or take them out of context. Many people have been misled by errant interpretations. The Bible warns against false teachers who distort God's truth (2 Peter 2:1–2), so we must be prepared and vigilant by examining God's Word for ourselves. "…if we neglect the Word of God and don't build it into our lives, when Satan comes along we're all too easily deceived."[49]

"Fundamentally, the gospel is the revelation of who God is and who we are, and how we can be reconciled to him. Yet in the American dream, where self reigns as king (or queen), we have the dangerous tendency to misunderstand, minimize and even manipulate the gospel in order to accommodate our assumptions and our desires. As a result, we desperately need to explore how much of our understanding of the gospel…is biblical."[50]

Intimacy with God is best cultivated by alone-time with Him. When we read God's Word for ourselves, we are better able to discern what it says in general, but more importantly, we see the specific application to our lives. "We should approach the Bible with a sense of submission, wanting to hear what the Living God has to say to us,"[51] not using it to reinforce our own beliefs. If the Bible seems too difficult to understand, try a more modern translation. The unique quality of the Bible is that it is "God breathed"—the actual living, inspired Word of God. Rather than just words on a page like another book, God uses Scripture to speak directly to us.

All Scripture is God-breathed and is useful for teaching,
rebuking, correcting and training in righteousness, so that the
servant of God may be thoroughly equipped for every good work.
(2 Timothy 3:16–17)

For the word of God is alive and active. Sharper than any double-
edged sword, it penetrates even to dividing soul and spirit, joints
and marrow; it judges the thoughts and attitudes of the heart.
(Hebrews 4:12)

Here are two examples of God using Scripture to speak to speak to people.

As a junior high student, Ed went through Lutheran Confirmation and committed his life to the Lord. He grew in his faith, and read through the Bible, praying that God would make Himself real to him. He felt isolated from friends who were not serious about their faith, and he became somewhat of a loner.

As a university student, he spent a summer working in the Adirondack Mountains, and attended an area church. The visiting pastor preached a four-week sermon series on the first and second commandments, as outlined by Jesus in Mark 12:30–31. Ed felt confident in his devotion to God—loving God with his heart, soul, mind and strength. But, on the fourth Sunday, when the pastor spoke about loving your neighbor as yourself, Ed said it was as though the Holy Spirit drilled the text into his mind, showing him that he was not loving his neighbors by ignoring them.

A few months later, when Ed was quickly walking across campus to the library, avoiding people as obstacles to his progress, God "zapped" him with a sudden spiritual awareness of His reality and love for him. Ed felt this was an answer to his prayer from his teen years, where he had asked God to make Himself real to him. God also gave him an intense awareness of His love for the people around Him on the sidewalk. This began a process of God healing him from his loner tendencies and giving him a heart for people. God's second commandment, presented in this sermon, was the catalyst to change Ed's life. God's Word is indeed living and powerful, and sharper than any two-edged sword, piercing even to the division of soul and spirit.

God spoke to me through the scriptures, guiding me and preventing a disastrous mistake. Military life requires frequent moves. Our family had left one duty station and were on our way to the next—one close to Perry's family. When we arrived, we spent time house hunting.

We found the perfect house, or so we thought. It had everything we needed and then some: fun extras like an elaborate playground on an over-sized lot, and even an indoor slide. Excitedly, we brought my mother-in-law to see our find. She hated it. In fact, she said that if we bought that house, she wouldn't come visit. I was devastated and angry, but I knew that causing family discord would be unwise.

In frustration, I turned to the scriptures, asking God to lead me to a solution. My daily reading brought me to Proverbs 15:22: "Plans fail for lack of counsel." I believe God was telling me that I needed to listen to my mother-in-law. We resumed our house search and found another home. It wasn't as unique, but it certainly was very nice and met our needs. My mother-in-law liked this one.

Later, we discovered that the first house was in a deteriorating, crime-ridden neighborhood that had become overrun with drugs and gangs. Businesses closed, property values plummeted, and schools were failing. The house we bought, however, was in one of the top school districts, and home values were escalating quickly. Our neighbors were terrific. Our family relationships flourished. How grateful we were, when it was time to move again, that we could make a substantial profit on our house. My mother-in-law later developed her own personal connection with Jesus because of our strengthened relationship. Listening to God and being obedient, even when it was difficult, blessed me and my family.

I want to get to know God better, but I've struggled. Perhaps you have too. I've tried Bible reading plans and was diligent for a few weeks, but soon stopped. It was dull, hard to understand and uninviting. I felt guilty. I'm not a very disciplined person. I tried again. I kept a calendar and checked off the days, hoping the evident progress would be a reward. That lasted a little longer. I missed some days, felt discouraged and quit again. Most Bible reading plans list the day you are supposed to read a given text. I deleted the dates. This helped assuage my guilt, but I was still inconsistent. So, I tried a new plan. This time I decided to use colored pencils to highlight certain topics. I learned about God's character, wisdom and what pleased and displeased Him. I had a ready reference for prophecies about Jesus's coming and end times. I catalogued salvation messages so I could tell others about Jesus. This worked better. I was quite proud of myself for keeping up, but the text still wasn't alive.

Why wasn't I finding life in the scriptures? My reading plans had been all about me accomplishing a task, checking a box. What was my motive? Was it to give me bragging rights as a very spiritual person? Was I looking for truth, so I could argue more persuasively? We need not read the Bible to find truth but to do truth.[52] Dr. Willard advises that "it is better in one year to have ten good verses transferred *into the substance of our lives* than to have every word of the Bible flash before our eyes."[53] We need to change the way we approach the Bible.

Several authors have suggested that we make ourselves part of the story we are reading. Imagine you are one of the characters. Replicate the actions. Mimic the words with parallel emotion. What would you be thinking, what would you feel, how are others reacting to you? This helps make the story tangible. Another idea is to pretend you are making a movie. What scenes would you include? Where would you pan in or out? What would the scenery and costumes look like? These exercises help bring the story to life and engage you.

Another technique to personalize Scripture and make it come alive was explained to me by Dr. Ron Brenning, a pastor at Grace Chapel in Englewood, CO. He pointed out that Jesus prayed Scripture at times such as his wilderness temptation and on the cross. As we read a text, we can follow Jesus's example and look for phrases that contain praise, thanksgiving, confession, supplication or petitions and pray these concepts back to God. This helps us actualize and internalize what we read.

I have also found that "writing Psalms" is inspiring. David uses several components in his songs to God, so I replicated these, following his patterns in various Psalms, but applying them to my situation. What characteristics of God impress me? How do these make me want to respond to Him? What troubles me and makes me feel overwhelmed, forsaken, unworthy or oppressed? How does God meet these needs? What areas of my life are out of sync with Him and what sins do I need to confess? I try to be honest with God and speak from my inner being, just like David does.

Our goal is not just reading Scripture in a disciplined manner, learning what it says and even applying it to our lives. "The right view of approaching scripture matters. Our goal should be knowing and communicating with God and learning all that He means us to know about Himself."[54]

The more we *know* God, the better we can *hear* God.[55] We submit to Him, laying aside our own prejudices, positions, opinions and plans, and open our minds to God's Spirit. When we become Christ-followers, we have the Holy Spirit dwelling inside us. His job is to teach us, lead us to truth, comfort us and help us. (John 14:16–17, 26) The Holy Spirit will make God's words become alive for us in a personal way, as we allow God to speak through His Word to us. This explains why the Bible is so relevant. Each time we read a passage, it may have a different application to our lives at that moment.

I was excited to discover this new way of studying the Bible. I acknowledged that it was truly God's living Word and asked Him to speak to me through it. I asked Him to give me wisdom, correct me and help me learn about His character. Suddenly, Bible reading came to life. Words leapt off the page as I realized in awe that Almighty God was speaking to me. Yes, Me! Bible reading was no longer a part of a to-do list or a way to be spiritually proud.

I also found it useful to keep a journal. After reading a text, I asked God to show me what He wanted me to know in those words. I responded to what I learned and wrote it down. I was surprised to learn things about God I didn't know. Sometimes, as I read, He corrected me. Sometimes it was comfort or encouragement that came. Many times, He reaffirmed His love, goodness, faithfulness, patience, and other amazing qualities.

Encountering God's presence in this quiet time drew me back to Him with enthusiasm. If I neglected this time, I missed it. People who haven't eaten in a long time actually lose their taste for food. Eating becomes repulsive to them. It's the same with Scripture reading—our daily bread of life. When we neglect partaking, it becomes unsavory. However, as we "eat" we begin to hunger for the very words of God.

When your words came, I ate them;
they were my joy and my heart's delight.
(Jeremiah 15:16)

I loved reading about the Jewish tradition of Shavuot (the celebration of the day the Torah was given) for children beginning school or "Bet Sefer"— The House of the Book. Their writing slates were smeared with honey. Children licked the honey from the slate, symbolizing the sweetness of God's words.[56]

How sweet are your words to my taste, sweeter than honey to my mouth!
(Psalm 119:103)

With our busy lives, many of us don't have the capability to set aside much undistracted time for God, reading the Bible and praying. We may consider this as an aside rather than a necessity. It's important to develop this as a habit in our daily routines, because this time with God puts the rest of our lives on the right track. Charles Stanley said,

"When we tell God we don't have time for Him, we are really saying we don't have time for life, for joy, for peace, for direction or for prosperity, because He is the source of all these…the time of meditation is God's time of equipping us in preparation for life."[57]

Satan will do everything he can to keep us from God's Word. We start by asking God to help us be victorious over the thwarting power of the evil one, requesting Him to show us where we can make time. We should consider this a priority and be willing. He may wake us up early or keep us from falling asleep, so we have time for Him. Be conscientious. If something is important to us, we will find a way to make it happen and work it into our schedules.

Begin with baby steps. Don't succumb to guilt. God will bless our efforts and lead us to ever greater encounters with Him. There are practical ways to start. Patricia Shirer suggests writing Scripture references on cards and placing them in highly visible places: the car dashboard, the refrigerator, the bathroom mirror.

We will be immersed in Scripture throughout the day.[58] This is an effective way to memorize Scripture too. When we "hide God's word in our hearts," He can remind us of those verses to encourage us, comfort us, teach us, help us or guide us, even when we don't have the Bible in front of us. "It is as if the Helper [the Holy Spirit], searches through the library stacks of [our] unconscious where all manner of information has been filed away and produces the particular 'It is written' needed for the moment of battle."[59]

I have hidden your word in my heart that I might not sin against you.
(Psalm 119:11)

Your word is a lamp for my feet, a light on my path.
(Psalm 119:105)

God reminded me of a Scripture passage I had read when I experienced a mini-crisis. I was devastated. I looked down at my left hand and realized that the diamond had fallen out of my wedding ring. Not only was it expensive to replace, but it had irreplaceable sentimental value. It occurred to me that I could pray about this problem. God indeed cares about the things that concern us: lost keys, wayward pets, stalled cars, etc. In 1 Peter 5:7, we are told to "cast all [our] anxiety on Him because He cares for [us]." As I prayed about the lost diamond, the parable of the lost coin came to mind (Luke 15:8–9). The woman in the story swept her house clean and eventually found the coin. So, I vacuumed carefully and then sifted through the dust. There it was! My husband and I celebrated because what was lost was found.

Even as a new Christian, God used Scripture stored deep in her mind to speak to Annette. In her last semester of school, she had no way to pay for her final bill. That's when she met her husband-to-be, David. He scratched off a check for $800.

David had been pursuing Annette and asked her to marry him, but her previous dating relationships had not turned out very well. She was not interested, but she prayed and prayed. She asked God to tell her what to do. She knew very little about the Bible, though she had read it once. On her knees beside her bed in her dorm room, a voice whispered in her ear: "Many claim to have unfailing love, but a faithful person who can find?" (Proverbs 20:6). God told her that David was a faithful man, and that she should marry him.

For those who are ready for a deeper Bible study program, that involves a more intense exposure, Dallas Willard presented a Scripture reading method which I have found to be helpful for hearing God in His Word. This method is called "Lectio Divina" defined on the internet as "a traditional Benedictine practice of scriptural reading, meditation and prayer intended to promote communion with God and to increase the knowledge of God's Word. It does not treat Scripture as texts to be studied, but as the Living Word."[60] Here is Dr. Willard's application of that practice:

1. *Lectio*: Read the passage slowly and carefully, considering the invitation that reading scripture is encountering God Himself or hearing His voice.
2. *Meditato*: Read the passage a second time, looking for a word or phrase that stands out for you. Ask God how this connects with your life.
3. *Oratio*: Read the passage one last time and talk to God about what you think the Spirit is saying to you.
4. *Contemplatio*: Contemplate the passage. What have you learned about God? Sit in companionship with Him and be with Him. Let Him speak to you.[61]

When I used Dr. Willard's plan, I was amazed. God revealed Himself to me even in the drier portions of Numbers and Leviticus. I learned about His attention to detail,

His remarkable organization, and His unfailing concern for His people. As I applied that to my own life, I saw how God is indeed sovereign and cares about each detail of my life. Understanding His character inspires me to trust Him more.

King David exhorts us to not only read Scripture, but also to meditate on it by quietly and purposefully spending time with God and His Word (Psalm 119:97). The word "meditate" sends up a red flag for some Christians who feel it correlates with some of the Zen-like practices of emptying one's mind to achieve a more enlightened state. I agree with Pricilla Shirer when she retorts that she is not about to let some pagan ritual steal a piece of her spiritual arsenal simply because it is subject to misuse. Meditation is not emptying our minds but placing concentrated focus on God and His Word.[62]

What we know *about* God becomes actually knowing God, and then putting this knowledge to use.[63] We need to sit quietly before the Lord, letting His truth make its full and proper impact on our mind and heart, reasoning through our own doubts, moods and problems in the light of His love, power and grace. We review how God has treated us and others in the past. We reflect on what we know about His character and promises, as revealed in His Word. The quieting effects of meditation help us find His direction and purpose for our lives.[64] When we do this, we see things from a new perspective. Our worry dissolves. Problems don't seem so big. The weight of our burdens is lessened, and we feel an all-encompassing sense of peace.

A Bible reading plan in which God is speaking to us personally can deepen and invigorate lifeless spiritual pursuits. "Once, the Bible was just so many words to us— 'clouds and darkness'—then suddenly, the words become spirit and life because Jesus speaks them to us."[65] If we find the Bible to be boring and irrelevant, we have not encountered the God of the Bible.[66] He is what engages us, as we develop a relationship with Him.

When you received the word of God, which you heard from us,
you accepted it not as a human word, but as it actually is, the
word of God, which is indeed at work in you who believe.
(1 Thessalonians 2:13)

"Hearing the voice of the Almighty has changed my humdrum Christian experience from a discipline into a passion. I no longer study the Bible as an instructional and theological tool (though it certainly is), but also as God's love letter to me."[67]

Stop and Refresh

1. Share about a time when you were driving and didn't stop to ask directions. Did you encounter difficulties? Have there been times in your faith walk where you have not sought directions? What happened?

2. Do you believe the Bible is God's inspired Word? Why or why not? What makes the Bible "come to life"?

3. Why is it important to read the Bible? Have you ever tried a Bible reading plan? Was it successful? Why or why not? What can you do to be more successful?

4. Write a psalm, patterning it after David's Psalms. If you are in a group study, share it with your group.

5. What should be our purpose in reading Scripture? Try "Lectio Divina" for a week. Try keeping a journal. Did this help you connect with the God of the Bible?

Chapter Seven

YOUR TRAVELING COMPANION

Getting to know God by spending time with Him

Be still and know that I am God.
(Psalm 46:10)

The dog barks, the phone rings, the kids yell, the doorbell dings. How can we shut out the din and spend quiet time getting to know our Father God?

On a road trip, especially if we travel in the summertime, we can expect road construction, delays and detours. Persistence is needed tackle torn up roads, tar smells and the loud staccato of jack hammers. Patience is required to handle imposed slow speeds that threaten our time lines. We want to hurry up and get there! Traveling like this can be stressful. Where is the joy of our journey?

Diversions threaten our progress toward God too. It's difficult to hear Him above the noise and make progress toward Him when things get in our way. We want to hurry, have our needs met and then get on with our lives. It is hard to linger in God's presence. Sometimes we feel guilty about making time for God, because we're needed elsewhere. The world is waiting to squeeze us into its mold and crowd out the time we try to devote to God, keeping us from doing the very thing that pleases Him the most —seeking His face.[68] Setting aside time for God can become stressful instead of joyful.

Spending time alone with God and getting to know Him through prayer is a vital step toward reaching our destination of a deeper relationship with God. We need persistence and patience to make this a priority. Setting aside moments for God puts the rest of our life on track. Through experience we will see how desperately we need this to function, and it will become our delight. Bill Hybels describes his twenty-year journey to understanding prayer in his book *Too Busy Not to Pray*. He says, "The greatest fulfillment has not been the list of miraculous answers to prayers I have received, although that has been wonderful. The greatest thrill has been the qualitative difference in my relationship with God."[69]

Our survey responders experienced interruptions and obstacles in their prayer lives too and addressed them creatively. Some get away from the chaos by taking a walk, jogging, or sitting outside to reflect on God in nature. Others play music to drown out the distractions or sing at the top of their lungs to set the stage. Cell phones are turned off. A room with a closed door is a good sanctuary and everyone around should know that we're not to be disturbed. A special place set aside for prayer—a prayer room or even a closet—can create a conducive atmosphere for God to interact with us.

Pastor Tim Johnson noted that prayer can revolve around movement too: biking, quilting, jogging, painting, hiking, gardening, etc. He hikes with his dog, Riley, in an open area behind his house. Sometimes when our bodies are involved in a physical activity it is easier to focus our minds. Tim says we all need to get away and be totally honest with God. "We all need a place where we can scream at the top of our lungs and no one will call the cops." God knows what we are thinking, is aware of our grief and discouragement and is ready to meet us where we are.[70]

However, even when I'm removed from noise and interruptions, my mind wanders. I think of my to-do list or the people I am praying about. Not being able to focus is so frustrating. This is a discipline that takes concentration and practice.

We demolish arguments and every pretension that sets
itself up against the knowledge of God, and we take
captive every thought to make it obedient to Christ.
(2 Corinthians 10:5)

When we pray, we need to keep God in the forefront, not hurriedly buzzing through our prayer list so we can be done with it. We come before God to get to know Him, and enter His presence, not just request things from Him. His Spirit in us teaches us and helps us understand who God is and how He works. Remember, Jesus wants to be our friend, so we shouldn't worry about whether or not we're doing prayer right. C. S. Lewis noted that "God may speak to us most intimately when He catches us off guard because our preparations to receive Him sometimes have the opposite effect."[71] Relax and enjoy His presence expectantly, without inhibitions. God knows us intimately, so we can't pretend before Him. He knows the best and the worst about us, forgiving the worst and nurturing the best. Prayer is a time where we develop our friendship with Jesus. We talk, and He listens, and He talks, and we listen. In prayer we enter the very presence of God and come into His throne room with confidence.

I've learned to begin my quiet time by asking God to focus my attention and speak to me, diminishing the stimulation of the world around me that competes with His presence. Satan must not steal this time, so I ask God to keep him at bay. I try to visualize God in His throne room and worship Him (Isaiah 6:1–4). Worship expands my mind to more deeply understand God's greatness, so I have more faith when I talk to Him about my problems. I talk out loud, imagining Him walking with me, listening. The truths I've learned in His Word are applied to my life by the Spirit. My prayer is: "Search me, O God, and know my heart; test me and know my anxious thoughts. See if there is any offensive way in me and lead me in the way everlasting" (Psalm 139:23–24). Developing this right heart attitude is crucial to effective prayers. The Bible instructs me to first deal with my sin, my unforgiveness toward others, and my doubt so that my prayer channel is open. Then, as I immerse myself in God's presence, I become more keenly aware of His love, goodness, majesty, faithfulness, sovereignty and power, enabling me to trust Him more. This helps me better face the challenges of my day.

Our prayer life needn't be confined to a few moments set aside for God in our quiet time. As we become more keenly aware of God's presence, we develop seeing eyes and hearing ears for what He wants to tell us and show us all day. "We should get in the habit of continually seeking His counsel on everything, instead of making our own commonsense decisions, and then asking Him to bless them. We are not told to 'walk in the light' of our conscience or in the light of a sense of duty, but to 'walk in the light *as He is in the light*.'"[72] There is no time in our day when God is irrelevant.

God showers us with blessings daily, but unless we are paying attention we won't perceive them.[73] Remain in "response mode" eagerly looking for Jesus's "sparkling surprises just around the bend."[74] In a walk with Him, there aren't coincidences. He often does new and unexpected things in our lives. We should aspire to "fix our eyes on Jesus" (Hebrews 12:1–2) all day, paying attention to what He is doing, and checking in with Him about what we are doing. Each pause in our day—waiting in line, on hold on the phone, stuck in traffic—can become an opportunity to connect with Jesus and learn to walk in His presence. This begins to develop our paradise-garden relationship.

Pastor Ron set his cell phone alarm to sound every hour. No matter what he is doing, he will stop and check in with God, saying a quick prayer, and asking God to guide him. Once when he was in a business meeting, his alarm sounded. He was embarrassed when the CEO asked him sarcastically if he needed to be somewhere else. "No," he said, "it's my reminder to pray." "Well, let's pray then," the CEO advised. Right in the middle of this meeting they stopped and prayed.

At first, it will be a continual effort to remain in God's presence, but as we train ourselves to abide—walking with Him continually—this will become a habit, an integral part of our lives. We'll abide in Him without any conscious effort.[75] We'll begin to realize that He is there all the time. Like Jacob, we can say, "Surely the Lord is in this place, but I was unaware of it" (Genesis 28:16). The concept of praying without ceasing becomes a reality, because we are always together with Him (1 Thessalonians 5:17). He sees everything we are doing, He hears our conversations, and He even understands our thoughts (Psalm 139:1–6). This can be both comforting and disconcerting. I am glad He is with me, and I have the comfort of knowing He guides and protects me, but it also makes me a little uneasy. Knowing He is watching reminds me to be more careful to obey His instructions, resist temptation, and do things that show His light and love.

Everything that we do and say can be guided and empowered by the Holy Spirit who dwells in us. In the Old Testament, God sent His spirit to inspire those who were working on the tabernacle so that they could do a superb job (Exodus 35:30–35). God's Spirit lives in us to help us be all we can be too. I have used this principle in my writing as I ask God to help and inspire me. As we remain in God's presence, whatever we are doing can be an act of worship-- our best work that brings glory and honor to Him, not ourselves. We live for the applause not of people, but of nail-scarred hands.[76]

"And whatever you do, whether in word or deed, do it all in the name of the Lord Jesus, giving thanks to God the Father through him."
(Colossians 3:17)

My son, Kurt, brought this idea home to me when his high school soccer team decided to play soccer as an act of worship—doing their best, behaving honorably and fairly, and giving the glory to God for each opportunity. Each time they stepped on the pitch (field) they dedicated the game to the Lord, and after every goal they pointed heavenward, giving Him the glory. God blessed their dedication with a state championship.

Because of the great mercy God has shown us, offer your lives as a living sacrifice to him—an offering that is only for God

and pleasing to him. Considering what he has done, it is only
right that you should worship him in this way.
(Romans 12:1 ERV)

Constant abiding in Jesus and doing everything for Him develops our paradise-garden relationship with God: ever talking to Him, ever worshipping, ever listening and becoming one with His Spirit. Jesus prayed that we would become one with the Father as He is one with the Father (John 17:20–21). This unity of spirit gives direction, power and purpose to our prayers.

Ask and You Will Receive

According to my survey results, the most common component of prayer is asking God for something for ourselves or others. The Bible assures us that God loves us and desires to give good gifts to His children (Matthew 7:9–11). As believers, we can come to God as children come to a loving Father. Ask and you shall receive (Matthew 21:22), we are told. The Bible lists several promises about asking and receiving, but many of them have conditions such as faith, righteousness, asking in Jesus's name, not harboring sin, and forgiving others. This is why it's so important to have the right heart attitude when we pray.

Therefore confess your sins to each other and pray for each other so that you
may be healed. The prayer of a righteous person is powerful and effective.
(James 5:16)

Faith is an especially important component of prayer. (James 1:6–7) We shouldn't throw our petitions at God's throne and dictate to Him how He should handle them, with the caveat that "Here it is, but I don't see how you are going to do this."[77] Be in touch with the mind of Christ. Listen more to God's Spirit and less to your doubts.[78] Faith comes by hearing God's Word (Romans 10:17), spending time with Him, and in our dependency, focusing on His greatness, goodness, and ability. We must come to the place where we don't just believe God theoretically in our minds, but "own" his truths in our hearts. Faith isn't something we just conjure up on our own, speaking "words of faith" to somehow solicit power and convince ourselves that we believe. Faith isn't the power in itself. Neither are our thoughts or words. When we pray in Jesus's name, faith activates His resurrection power, so that our empty hand can reach out to God in expectation.[79] Instead of focusing on what we want from God, we focus on God. We may want Him to "move the mountain into the sea," but He may in fact be planning to obliterate the mountain altogether. Let Him have His way, and have faith that by His Spirit, He will work in and through us for our good and His glory (Romans 8:28).

The good news is that only a little faith is enough, and God is in the position to even help our unbelief (Mark 9:24).[80] Jesus said that faith the size of a tiny mustard seed can move a mountain (Matthew 17:20). We can ask anything in Jesus's name and it will be done according to His will, so that our joy may be made complete (John 16:24). He doesn't withhold any good thing (Psalm 84:11) nor does He give us stones when we ask for bread (Matthew 7:7–11).[81] He doesn't play games with us, dangling a prize and making us come up with the right formula to receive it. Out of love for us, He offers us His best.

We have the tendency to do everything ourselves first, then pray as a last resort saying, "All I can do now is pray." Prayer should be our first response, not our last resort.[82] We shouldn't sell God short. "It is as false as it is irreverent to accuse God of forgetting, or overlooking, or losing interest in, the state and needs of His own people. If you have been resigning yourself to the thought that God has left you high and dry, seek grace to be ashamed of yourself. Such unbelieving pessimism deeply dishonors our great God and Saviour."[83] God loves us, is involved with us and in His majesty and power is able to do anything (Matthew 19:26). Bill Hybels comments that "You won't believe the changes that will occur in your life—in your marriage, your family, your career, your health, your ministry, your witnessing—once you are convinced in the core of your being that God is willing, that He is able and that He has invited you to come before His throne and do business in prayer."[84]

Ray Vander Laan told the story of Joshua and the people of Israel who approached the Jordan River, intending to cross. It was at flood stage. The priests, carrying the heavy ark of the covenant, started down the steep, slippery banks, followed by the entire nation of Israel. How in the world would they get across that rushing water? Yet, they didn't hesitate. They stepped out in faith believing in the power of God. The Bible tells us that the Jordan River was stopped and they all crossed on dry land—but *not until their feet touched the water.* (Joshua 3:15–16)[85] Make every effort to be attuned to the prompting of the Spirit, understand His leading and then step out with confidence in faith believing. We must step. We must act. "Praying can be 'dangerous business.' If [we] ask for piano lessons, [we'll] have to do some practicing."[86]

Fred told me about a word picture he received from God in which a shallow, muddy stream was bordered by two very arid berms. People were walking in the water but complaining about getting muddy. Fred believes this meant that if we want God's blessings (water) in this parched world, we'll need to get our feet dirty—step out, act and obey.

God wants us to pray, then work in tandem with Him to accomplish His purposes. We don't sit back and do nothing, waiting for God to do it all, but in our efforts, we must rely on His direction instead of our own plans. "We pray as if everything depends on God. We work as if everything depends on us."[87]

2 Chronicles 13–16 tells the story of Abijah, King of Judah, who went to battle against Jeroboam, King of Israel. They were brave and ready to fight valiantly but were greatly outnumbered: two to one. Jeroboam's forces surrounded Judah's army, but Abijah cried out to the Lord and God delivered Judah in spite of the odds. Verse 18 says: "the men of Judah were victorious because they relied on the Lord." Asa, Abijah's son then became king of Judah. He also relied on the Lord in battle and was victorious—the first time (14:11–13, 15:15). However, later in his life, he took matters into his own hands and formed a treaty with the King of Aram, thinking this would help him be successful against his enemies. God told him he had done a foolish thing, and He withdrew His support from him. (16:7–9) Instead of repenting, Asa became angry with God. He was afflicted with a disease of his feet, but still didn't seek God. (16:12). The remainder of his reign was plagued by wars (16:9).

It is important to learn from this example. If we wish to be successful in our requests, we must depend on God and seek Him in all our affairs, big or small, then follow His advice by working diligently. In our way of thinking, dependence on anything is considered immaturity. Self-sufficiency is valued.

In God's eyes, however, dependence on Him is a measure of spiritual maturity and wisdom.[88] We can't ignore God most of the time and come to Him when we are desperate and expect His answer. When He speaks, we must listen and obey with alacrity.

Penny and her family learned the importance of listening to God, and not choosing their own way when they were selling their home and buying a new house. They thought they had sold their home, but at the last minute their buyers backed out. Now they didn't have the money to buy the new house unless they borrowed it, taking on two house payments. They had already registered their kids in the new school, so Penny talked her mother into loaning them the money against her will. They prayed so much about the move, but God kept telling them, "no." Penny wanted that new house and thought their fervent prayers would change God's mind, but He was trying to keep them out of a mess. They didn't listen and followed their own plans.

It was a disaster. The kids got involved in cross-city busing and the house was built on bad soil, literally falling apart. They had double house payments since it took forever for their former house to sell. Penny pushed her agenda, even though she knew in her heart this was against what God was saying. They learned a big lesson. When God says no, listen!

When we are serious about prayer, we not only develop a deeper relationship with God, but we experience His "prevailing power."[89] We approach God boldly, claiming His promises as outlined in Scripture. He helps, He heals, He works. If you are willing to invite God to involve himself in your daily challenges, you will experience his prevailing power.... It may come in the form of wisdom, courage, confidence, perseverance or an attitude change. It may even be manifested in changes to circumstances and outright miracles. "God's prevailing power is released in the lives of people who pray."[90]

"A 'prayer warrior' is a person who is convinced that God is omnipotent—that God has the power to do anything, to change anyone and to intervene in any circumstance. A person who truly believes this refuses to doubt God."[91]

Pray Specifically

Many of us are uncomfortable with asking for our needs boldly, and shy away, thinking God is too busy to grant every minor request, or that it is selfish to ask Him for little things. Let's save our prayer power for the big stuff. The word *ask* actually means beg (John 16:24). As we realize the magnitude of our needs before God, not just in a physical, but in a spiritual sense, we can acknowledge our spiritual poverty and plead like a pauper, totally dependent on God and His goodness.[92] Jesus said, "Blessed are the poor in spirit for theirs is the kingdom of God" (Matthew 5:3). When we pray in personal deficiency, in total humbleness before God, His whole kingdom is at our disposal.

We may be skeptical about whether or not God will answer particular prayers, or fearful that we will be disappointed, so a less definite prayer is safer. Thus we pray only, "Your will be done—whatever you say, Lord"—in very general terms. Jesus specifically asked the blind man, "What do you want me to do for you?" (Mark 10:51). We should honestly tell Him what we need. He even cares about the little stuff. He is ready to help and heal. "Ask anything in my name and I will do it" (John 14:14).

Bernadette told me that, as a widow, she has experienced God's covering and protection through faith and prayer. One thing she has prayed about is her car. Prayer answers are the only way she can explain so few repairs on a car that is now over 355,000 miles.

She was driving with her son through Nebraska, home to Colorado, in a snow storm. In the middle of nowhere the car stopped, right in the center of the road. It would not start in drive, so she prayed for the Lord's help. She put it in first gear and amazingly it started. They drove a hundred miles to Sydney, Nebraska, in fourth gear without stopping.

She was afraid it would stall again, and it did, in the middle of an intersection. She said, "Oh, Lord, what can I do?" Her son sitting next to her said, "Pray, Mom," and yes, she did. She tried to start it in first gear again, but it made a horrible grinding noise. She put it in drive again praying God's grace would cover this. It started!

They drove the remaining two hundred miles to Denver with no problems. Later her mechanic said the crank shaft wiring was stripped and he wasn't sure how in the world they had made it home. When she told him God had answered their prayers, he said, "I think I have to go with that story."

God wants to meet all our needs. In times of trouble, focus on God's adequacy, not our own inadequacy. When we only pray in general, we never have the excitement of seeing specific prayers answered. In fact, we may hardly recognize an answer when it comes. It's "important to get God's guidance on pinpointing where and how He wants His supply to come to us."[93] We should ask for wisdom that makes God's desires clear, removing selfishness from the equation, but pray specifically for our needs, joyously experiencing God's miraculous outcomes.

Lisa Steven, the executive director of Hope House of Colorado, has experienced numerous answers to prayer as they pour out their concerns before God and then watch Him work in miraculous ways. Hope House offers self-sufficiency programs for parenting teen moms, including a residential program, GED and college program, and classes such as parenting, Bible study, and budgeting.

Lisa recently shared a story with me about a time in 2009 when finances were tight. The recession had dried up a sizable amount of their donations since people in their own financial difficulties could no longer give. She had made numerous cuts to the budget and was now faced with diminishing their residency program.

One of the volunteers enthusiastically entered her office, saying that she had met two homeless teens with toddlers in a park. "We have to take them in!" the volunteer said. Lisa thought, "How in the world can we accept more residents when we can't even support what we have?" The girls had nowhere else to go, so with faith for God's provision, Lisa relented.

The next Sunday in church, Lisa was thinking about Hope House's financial problems, praying for God's intervention. She was envisioning a massive check, so God's answer surprised her. In His still small voice He said to her, "Use what I have already given you."

She didn't know what this meant, but as the week unfolded, volunteers began coming "out of the woodwork." Even paid staff that she had had to let go, came to help. With the strong volunteer work force, they were able to function on a much lower budget, keeping the residency program open and housing the extra girls. These two girls eventually gave their lives to Jesus and were changed from the inside out. One of the girls named Tina, sent this note: "Hope House is a constant reminder that everything will be okay. Sometimes you can forget that God is there. Then you come to Hope House and are reminded of Him and His goodness."

God indeed is willing and ready to answer our requests and help us in our times of need. Come to Him in prayer. He will do amazing things.

You do not have because you do not ask it of God. You ask God for something and do not receive it, because you ask with wrong motives out of selfishness or with an unrighteous agenda.
(James 4:3 AMP)

Delight yourself also in the Lord, And
He shall give you the desires of your heart.
(Psalm 37:4 NKJV)

Nora shared a story about her eighteen-month-old daughter, Hester. She got ahold of an iron tablet bottle and ate all sixty tablets. Two different doctors, who had not collaborated, said the baby would die that night. She was given an experimental medication and spent several days in intensive care. People all over were praying for Hester's recovery via prayer chains. The doctors could not explain why she lived. Babies taking a much lesser dose had died. Everyone involved felt they had witnessed a true miracle.

My husband, Perry, received last-minute U.S. Army orders to leave Ft. Benning, Georgia and go to Wheaton College in Illinois to teach ROTC. We had a house to sell. Quickly. Our Realtor shook her head at the impossibility. "Houses take at least three months to sell," she told us. We had two weeks. Our house had to sell so we could purchase a place in Wheaton. We didn't have a financial buffer. For almost two weeks, no one even came to look. On the last weekend, before Perry went to Wheaton to house-hunt, we decided to leave town while the Realtor had an open house. On our way out the door, we stood in our entryway and prayed, "God, please have someone come to buy the house. When they walk in the door, let them feel like it's home." I don't know why we prayed that way, but when we returned late Sunday afternoon, our Realtor met us at the door grinning. Only one person had come. He stepped inside the door and said, "This place feels like home." He didn't even tour the house. He signed the contract immediately.

This amazing experience continued as Perry arrived in Wheaton. We had prayed for a house close to campus with an extra room, so we could have a live-in student, a fenced yard for our dogs, and a fireplace to brave the cold. Perry found houses to be much more than we could afford. In discouragement, we prayed. He saw an ad in the paper for a home "For Sale by Owner." It was listed at a price beyond our budget, but he went to look anyway. The owner, a retired missionary, had put out a "fleece" (Judges 6:35–40), asking God to clearly show him His will. He had listed the house for just one day, not sure that he wanted to sell. If he sold, he wanted the buyer to be someone working at the college.

He dropped the price significantly to be within our budget. He took on the mortgage himself, saving us hundreds of dollars in closing costs and offering us an interest rate well below the going rate. (At that time it was 17 percent!) The house was a mile from campus. It had an extra room to house a student. But where were the fenced yard and fireplace? The money we saved in closing costs was the same amount required to install a chain link fence. When I mentioned the fireplace to the owner, he laughed. "You should have prayed for a fireplace that worked!" He had bricked up the fireplace in the living room because it was too drafty.

God has not changed from the God of the Bible (Malachi 3:6, Hebrews 13:8). He still does marvelous things. He is willing and able to do what His people—you and I—need! We can be assured that what He has promised He is also able to perform (Romans 4:21).

And whatever we ask we receive from Him, because we keep His commandments and do those things that are pleasing in His sight.
(1 John 3:22 NKJV)

When We Don't Know How to Pray

Have you ever been clueless about how to pray for a particular person, or even how to pray about a need you have yourself? We know that God knows the situation even better than we do, and we can trust His Spirit to pray for us.

> *Also, the Spirit helps us. We are very weak, but the Spirit*
> *helps us with our weakness. We don't know how to pray as we*
> *should, but the Spirit himself speaks to God for us. He begs*
> *God for us, speaking to him with feelings too deep for words.*
> (Romans 8:26 ERV)

When I walk my dog by a nearby lake, I like to pray. One morning, I was praying for a woman I knew who had multiple physical, mental, emotional and spiritual problems. Her needs were so vast that I didn't know how to pray for her, so I asked God to show me, remembering the verse in Romans 8 that says the Holy Spirit intercedes for us when we don't know how to pray.

Suddenly, I was "transported" in a realistic vision to her home. She was sitting on her couch with demons all around her—sitting next to her, on her head and shoulders, by her feet and even outside, looking in the windows. Some had their fingers stuck in her head and back. I could see that they were causing her pain and discomfort. I asked their names and they began introducing themselves: Pain, Fear, Depression, Doubt, Sickness, Anxiety, Hopelessness, etc. Then I was back at the lake with my dog. I was shaken. Certainly, this was the result of an overactive imagination and reading too much Frank Peretti.

I argued with God about this for the rest of the day. Of course, I wouldn't say anything about this because it was just too weird, and people would think I was crazy. That afternoon, I shopped at a department store and went to the restroom. Suddenly I heard a loud, authoritative voice that said, "When you ask for bread, would I give you a stone?" I immediately realized that I had asked God to show me how to pray and He had. "Okay, Lord. I will be obedient in sharing this, even if people think I'm irrational."

First, I brought it up to my Bible Study group, asking them to pray with me for courage and discernment. They didn't think it was weird. They laid hands on me and prayed. We all experienced a very definite awareness of the forces of evil and called upon Jesus to be victorious and protect us from Satan and his demons. Empowered by their prayers and the Holy Spirit, I got up the courage to confront my friend—the woman for whom I had prayed. She also didn't think this was ridiculous, and this struck a chord of truth with her. She told me she had suspected her house was haunted because weird things kept happening—strange noises, doors shutting, things moving. I didn't feel adequate to pray against these demons with her by myself, so she went to her minister and told him the story. He and his associates prayed for her, also believing in the veracity of this. For the first time in a long time she felt peace. She even moved out of her house. Though she still experiences some problems, she has mostly been released from this horrible oppression. Thank God for showing me how to pray and giving me the courage to speak.

Many of us are uncomfortable with the idea of demons and find it hard to believe they exist. This partially explains my trepidation in talking about this. Throughout the New Testament, however, Jesus often cast out demons that were possessing and oppressing people, causing them to do and experience great harm. The disciples and Paul also encountered demons, and were able with God's power to get rid of them, "because the Spirit who is in you is more powerful than the spirit in those who belong to the world" (1 John 4:4 GNT). We even see evidence of the influence of evil spirits in the Old Testament when they came upon King Saul, and thwarted the messengers coming to Daniel. There is extensive evidence that they are active in our time as well, so ask God to help you discern and open your spiritual eyes. "For we do not wrestle against flesh and blood, but against principalities, against powers, against the rulers of the darkness of this age, against spiritual *hosts* of wickedness in the heavenly *places"*(Ephesians 6:12 NKJV).

Sometimes God doesn't reveal the situation to us, and we have to trust Him to meet the needs in His way. When we pray with the help of the Holy Spirit, we can be assured that the prayers are the right ones, and that they will be powerful.

> *I am amazed, Lord, at the powerful things you did in*
> *the past. Now I pray that you will do great things in our*
> *time. Please make these things happen in our own days.*
> (Habakkuk 3:2 ERV)

——•◦ *Stop and Refresh* ◦•——

1. Have you been successful in finding a way to block out distractions when you try to spend time with God? Share your advice.

2. Do you believe that when we pray we enter the very presence of God? Why or why not? If this is true, how does this impact your prayer life?

3. Read 1 Thessalonians 5:16–18. What does it mean to pray continually (without ceasing)?

4. What are some important components of prayer? Why is it important to have faith and not doubt? How do we do that? What is our part in prayer? What is God's part?

5. What does it mean to pray according to God's will or the mind of Christ? Does this mean we can't pray for our specific needs, but only God's will? How does the Holy Spirit help us pray?

Chapter Eight

IN THE FOG

When God is silent

*Please, Lord, look down from your holy and glorious home in the heavens
and see what's going on. Have you lost interest? Where is your power? Show
that you care about us and have mercy!*
(Isaiah 63:15 CEV)

We've seen the power of God and believe that He can and will do anything. He is mighty to save. But, praying specifically for something can be extremely frustrating. We ask and ask and don't get what we want. The lack of answered prayer was the number one cause of people's frustration with prayer, as indicated in their survey responses. I was moved by the pain that surfaced in the words of those who were in devastating circumstances but could not see or hear God. When God doesn't answer in our way and our time, we might turn from Him in anger, feeling that He has forsaken us.

We all experience times when God's presence isn't evident. When the nation of Israel was in the desert, all they saw on Mt. Sinai was a cloud. God's amazing work of writing His laws on stone tablets was obscured for a long time. They gave up on Him and built their own god—a golden calf (Exodus 32). We also often live in the fog of our unknowing, where divine realities are veiled. In times like these, instead of giving up and turning to our own form of idols—our self-sufficiency—we must carefully be watching for little flashes of light that give us a peek into the extraordinary presence, work and influence of Christ.[94]

God's silence in our time of need is disconcerting. King David experienced this and wrote in the Psalms, "Why, Lord, do you stand far off? Why do you hide yourself in times of trouble?" (Psalm 10:1). The Holy Spirit may lead us into a wilderness, as He did Jesus (Matthew 4:1). We thirst, we hunger, we don't see or hear God and feel abandoned. Like the Israelites wandering in the desert, we murmur and complain and may miss our personal "Promised Land"— the things God is trying to teach us and show us.[95] "He may be about to use this dry or dreadful season in [our] life as the catalyst to reveal an important, relevant message to [us]."[96] A friend likened these times of silence to taking an examination. The proctor stays quiet and doesn't talk while we are testing. Yet, she never leaves. She has equipped us with the information and now wants us to discover answers.

Like the proctor, God never leaves us or forsakes us (Deuteronomy 31:6). Even when we don't sense His presence, He is there. It is a mistake to feel abandoned and unloved when difficulties enter our lives. Don't let your grief, bitterness or anxiety insulate you from God's healing power and peace.[97] Don't hide in the dark corner of anguish and self-pity. God is always working, helping and even carrying us. The poem *Footprints in the Sand* by Mary Stevenson depicts a single set of footprints in sand which causes dismay because God seems absent when He is most needed. Instead He replies, "When you saw only one set of footprints, it was then that I carried you."[98]

A friend saw firsthand how God carried her through a tough situation. At seventy-seven, she was struggling with a few health problems— cataracts and a pacemaker. Her husband was diagnosed with dementia, could no longer drive and needed enhanced care. Her one-hundred-year-old mother was living with her. She had a large house and yard which demanded work. She decided she had to move, and she had to navigate all of this herself, making all the decisions and downsizing from fifty-four years of accumulated stuff and memories. Everything was up to her. She was overwhelmed and stressed, but she had to stay strong.

My friend needed help. She needed Jesus! As she looks back, she sees this year as the personification of the "Footsteps in the Sand." She could feel God holding her, pushing her forward. If she started down the wrong path, God corrected her. God provided as much help from friends as was needed, not more. Her cataracts were removed without complications. She moved into a retirement community where she immediately felt love and support.

She wrote, "I never could have gotten through this year without my God. I didn't feel the least bit selfish taking up so much of His time. He wants to walk with us every minute of every day. When we let Him do that, living is so much easier. We may not have everything, but we will always have what we need, becoming the person God wants us to be."

God's response to our prayers is often not an immediate resolution. Although we are told to make requests, we should use our prayer time to seek God's presence, not just His presents; the Giver, not just His gifts. We can't treat God like a big genie in the sky who should grant our wishes immediately, or a cosmic butler that should clean up our messes. There are no tricks or gimmicks to get what we want from God—no surefire technique to squeeze what we want out of Him.[99] Are our prayers a dictation to God instructing Him what He must do? When we seek God only for what He will give us, His blessings become idols in our hearts.[100] We make the mistake of aligning God to our desires rather than aligning ourselves to His desires for us.

When we shift our praying to getting to know God rather than getting something from Him, our prayers become more meaningful and purposeful. C. S. Lewis describes prayer as "letting one's mind run up the sunbeam to the sun."[101] God is our focus. He changes the desires of our hearts to His will, so we can pray specifically according to His will and not our own. Our "wish list" must be controlled by God.[102] We begin to see a bigger eternal picture, above our own immediate wants and circumstances. He might grant our requests, but He also might say "no" or "wait."

What do we do when God says, wait? This is one of the toughest challenges we face in our prayer time. We want God to work immediately, we want to see His hand, we want to hear His voice. "God's timing is rarely our own, but it is always worth waiting for."[103] It's in the waiting that He develops perseverance and persistence in us, and we learn to trust Him, walking by faith and not by sight (2 Corinthians 5:7).

> *[Woe] to those who say, "Let God hurry; let him hasten his*
> *work so we may see it. The plan of the Holy One of Israel—*
> *let it approach, let it come into view, so we may know it."*
> (Isaiah 5:19)

> *Be still before the Lord and wait patiently for him.*
> (Psalm 37:7)

While we wait, it is easy to worry. Worry is not an indication of how astute we are, but an indication of how sinful we are. We underestimate the power of God and become fixed on the culmination of our own plans, determined to have our own way.[104] We question God. We pace up and down twiddling our thumbs, looking at the clock. Our sleep suffers, and our appetite is either diminished or increased as we nibble mindlessly. Our blood pressure rises. All kinds of health concerns are attributed to stress. And, then, we snap at people in our lives, and our relationships begin to suffer too. It is no secret that worry is destructive. God wants us to give it all to Him, and not worry. He is the author of inner peace, and as we wait, He will teach us to rely completely on Him.

Do not be anxious about anything, but in every situation, by prayer and petition, with thanksgiving, present your requests to God. And the peace of God, which transcends all understanding, will guard your hearts and your minds in Christ Jesus.
(Philippians 4:6–7)

George Müller, the director of an orphanage in England in the late nineteenth century, learned the importance of waiting on God. In his book *Answers to Prayer,* he cited time after time when he prayed and had to wait until the very last minute for God's response. He never had a cupboard full of food or a padded bank account. When he needed food for the children's table, they sat down and prayed over their empty plates. The doorbell would ring, and there were provisions. If he needed money, a check would arrive in the mail just as the bill was due—never before. He learned to wait peacefully on God, trusting in His faithfulness to provide. Here is one story of many.

"One morning, all the plates and cups and bowls on the table were empty. There was no food in the larder and no money to buy food. The children were standing, waiting for their morning meal, when Müller said, 'Children, you know we must be in time for school.' Then lifting up his hands he prayed, 'Dear Father, we thank Thee for what Thou art going to give us to eat.'

There was a knock at the door. The baker stood there, and said, 'Mr. Müller, I couldn't sleep last night. Somehow I felt you didn't have bread for breakfast, and the Lord wanted me to send you some. So I got up at 2 a.m. and baked some fresh bread, and have brought it.'

Mr. Müller thanked the baker, and no sooner had he left, when there was a second knock at the door. It was the milkman. He announced that his milk cart had broken down right in front of the orphanage, and he would like to give the children his cans of fresh milk so he could empty his wagon and repair it."[105]

George Müller describes his experiences this way:

"The Lord was saying by this poverty, "I will now see whether you will truly lean upon me, and whether you will truly look to me..." The more I am in a position to be tried in faith ... the more shall I have opportunity of seeing God's help and deliverance, and every fresh instance, in which He helps and delivers me, will tend towards the increase of my faith... Therefore, the believer should not shrink from situations, positions, circumstances in which his faith may be tried, but should cheerfully embrace them as opportunities where he may see the hand of God stretched out on his behalf."[106]

God acts, but He doesn't *always* do so immediately. Sometimes He wants us to wait and trust, building our faith in the waiting. I remember a time when I became very impatient with God and upset that He wasn't acting quickly enough.

We put our house on the market, needing to move because of Perry's disability. We found a house we liked in our daughter's neighborhood. The seller wouldn't accept a contingency, and the bank wouldn't give us a bridge loan. I prayed, "Lord, help our house sell quickly so we can buy that house." Our house didn't sell. Someone else bought "our" intended house. I was frustrated. We ended up taking our house off the market. When I prayed, somewhat angry with God, He spoke to my mind saying, "Do you want to settle, or do you want my best?" Two years later, we again listed our house. The market had improved dramatically, and our house sold quickly, making a better profit. We found a beautiful lot with a view and had a handicapped-accessible home built to our specifications with everything that we needed. Now that we live in this new home, I have often felt, "Yes, this is God's best, worth waiting for."

In our impatience, we must actively be in His presence, so we can endure. When God seems far off, we should keep our antennae up for even the faintest glimmer of His presence.[107] It helps to remain engaged while we wait. "Until God opens the next door, praise Him in the hallway."[108] Praise brings peace. Thanksgiving moves our thoughts from ourselves to a mighty God who is there and is our immovable rock, capable of solving any problem. Here are some strategies for waiting.[109]

Be Thankful: Thankfulness is the best way to draw close to God because it opens our hearts to rich communication with Him.[110] Talk to God, thank Him and praise Him, turning your thoughts from your problems to His boundless love, grace and power. Thank Him for the answers He has set in motion long before we see the results,[111] always giving thanks to God the Father for everything, in the name of our Lord Jesus Christ" (Ephesians 5:20). Being thankful transforms our hearts to better hear and see God's work, and then be able to show His light to others. Complaining tarnishes our light. Let's shine! (Philippians 2:15)

Sing: God doesn't need our praise, but we need to praise Him to grow closer to Him and focus on His greatness. Through song, we can be "taken away to another world" to reflect on His great love and mercy. Music has a way of lightening our loads and lifting our spirits. We do this as a "sacrifice of praise" even when we don't feel like it. "Let us continually offer to God a sacrifice of praise—the fruit of lips that openly profess his name" (Hebrews 13:15).

Offer it Up: We can make a conscious effort to give our trouble to the Lord, placing it at His feet for His attention and use. The pain is still there, but something is added—a contentment comes in knowing the pain could make a difference in our lives. Ah, redemptive suffering. This means that even when we don't understand, offering it up to God gives it meaning.

> *Let us be thankful, then, because we receive a kingdom that*
> *cannot be shaken. Let us be grateful and worship God in a*
> *way that will please Him, with reverence and awe.*
> (Hebrews 12:28 GNT)

I liked Bill Hybels's description of prayer and answers:

If the request is wrong, God says, "No".

If the timing is wrong God says, "Slow."

If you are wrong, God says, "Grow."

But if the request is right, the timing is right, and you are right, God says, "Go!"[112]

———◆ *Stop and Refresh* ◆———

1. Share a time when you felt God was silent. Why do you think He seemed silent? What do you think He was doing? Are you frustrated with prayer or with God? Read Isaiah 57:11. When God seems silent, does it negatively affect our relationship to Him?

2. What are some reasons why prayers aren't being answered the way you had hoped? Why is it important to seek God and not just His gifts? How can our prayers become "idols?"

3. Read James 4:2–3. Why is it important to let God control our "wish list"?

4. What is the purpose of waiting for God's answer? How can we wait without being anxious?

5. It is said that "God helps those who help themselves." Do you think this is a valid statement? Why or why not? Read Deuteronomy 31:6–8. Do God's words to Moses and the nation of Israel apply to us today? Do you believe this? If this is true, what does this mean to you?

Chapter Nine

ROAD BLOCK
When God says no

*My tears have been my food day and night, while
people say to me all day long, "Where is your God?"*
(Psalm 42:3)

I had the privilege of joining in prayer for a friend who had pancreatic cancer. God dramatically healed her. A few months later, another friend was also diagnosed with pancreatic cancer. I prayed and prayed and pleaded with God to heal him. For a time, he made progress, but then took a turn for the worst. The family ended his life-support on Christmas Eve. I vividly remember getting the call from them while I was shopping at the grocery store. I stood in the aisle sobbing. For months after that I was angry with God and couldn't pray. I have no idea why God didn't answer our prayers and allowed this friend to die, while the other had been healed. It seemed so senseless. But, after a while, I began a journey back to God. I'm realizing that I don't have to make sense of these terrible situations or understand why God works the way He does. God wants my trust in His love and goodness in spite of the circumstances. "His understanding no one can fathom" (Isaiah 40:28).

The hardest times in our prayer life and journey to God are when He doesn't seem to be answering our prayers. Although God loves to give good gifts to His children, His primary concern is not our comfort. His idea of what's good for us doesn't always correspond with our idea of what's good for us. We usually want ease, pleasure, success, healing and blessings, and He gives us those sometimes. But, He wants us to grow up spiritually, having strong faith, and depending on Him completely. Thus, He might say no to our requests. Our troubles may be the bridge that God wants us to cross to get to the next phase of our lives.[113] Wisdom shows us that there is a balance of joy and sorrow. "Those who pursue the wisdom of God will arrive, despite troubles, at joy."[114]

In the garden of Gethsemane, Jesus asked God to remove this cup but He also prayed, "But do what you want, not what I want." (Matthew 26:36–46 ICB). It is okay to ask for relief and expect God to answer out of His love, mercy and goodness. Our faith in God, even if it is tiny—only the "size of a mustard seed,"—can "move mountains" (Matthew 17:20), and we can experience miraculous answers to prayer, "removing the cup." We shouldn't spiritualize our problems, bowing down before them in acquiescence to the will of God.[115] God is in the business of mountain moving, and is a practical, merciful God of grace who trumps our shortcomings and acts with power on our behalf. It is His Holy Spirit in us that guides us and gives us the faith we need to trust God as we ask Him to "remove this cup."

But we must be willing to submit to Him when the answer is not what we'd hoped—not my will, but yours. Submitting to God's will isn't resignation—barren of faith and blinded to the love of God—a place where we have no heart to rebel so we lay quietly down in the godless dust of the universe and steel ourselves for the worst.[116] We can't control our circumstances, but we can relax, trusting that God is in control and that in His love He knows what He is doing. Who are we to determine what is good or bad for us? We can't see the whole picture like God can. Acceptance leaves the door of hope wide open for God's creative plans,[117] which are better than what we imagine.

When we don't know how we ought to pray, we can turn our problems over to the Lord, asking His Spirit to intercede for us according to God's will (Romans 8:26–27). Jesus reminds us that He endured the cross for the "joy set before Him" (Hebrews 12:2). We also can endure what comes our way, realizing that there is joy set before us as well. We can be assured that God will use whatever happens for a purpose that accomplishes our good and His glory (Romans 8:28).

Our first tendency in problems is to complain, asking God to change the situation and remove the obstacle. We get frustrated and angry when He doesn't. What if the very thing we are trying to get rid of is what God is using to make us better and stronger? In her song "Blessings," Laura Story underscores this point. Blessings can come through raindrops and tears. Sleepless nights can let us know that God is near. Our disappointments and trials become "God's mercies in disguise."[118]

When difficulties come, there are two common opinions. In the first, people attribute suffering to our fallen, sinful world. God allows free will and that causes trouble. Unbelievers are not recipients of the righteousness and promises that God offers to believers through Jesus, and are still imprisoned by sin, alienated from the power and work of God. Since they refuse to acknowledge God, the bulk of evil in our world is the result of Him giving them over to their evil desires and actions (Romans 1:21–32; Galatians 3:22) and letting them do as they please. For believers, however, God does have the power to turn that trouble into good. We, as believers, are still in a world tainted by sin, but God can take that evil and turn it into a door of hope for us.[119] His business is to fix the brokenness caused by sin. He heals, He helps. Although He allows trouble to proliferate because of sin, it is not His choice.

In the second opinion, people think God is angry, judgmental and vindictive and will take every opportunity to zap us to get us back in line. He punishes sin and He punishes us. This makes us fear God and hope He will leave us alone. This is not the kind of relationship God wants us to have with Him. Though God does discipline us occasionally, He does so out of love, because He is refining us (Hebrews 12: 4–12). Sometimes He lets us experience the negative consequences of our own poor choices. Sometimes, by His grace, He preserves us from them.

But ultimately, He is judgmental, and if we want a good life we had better follow God's precepts.

> *For I command you today to love the* LORD *your god, to walk in obedience to him, and to keep his commands, decrees and laws; then you will live…I have set before you life and death, blessings and curses. Now choose life, so that you and your children may live and that you may love the Lord your God, listen to his voice, and hold fast to him. For the Lord is your life.*
> (Deuteronomy 30:16–20)

Although there is truth in both these positions, I don't think either of them adequately describes God's role in the suffering of His children. God treats those who acknowledge Him and belong to His family differently than others, because we do have access to His promises and have the Holy Spirit living in us. The Bible shows us that God is sovereign and in control. He has formed us and has a unique purpose for each of us as believers that includes shaping, molding and refining. God uses inward and outward pains to wean us from compromise and disobedience. He desires our love to be detached from earthy things and attached firmly on Him.[120] In the pressures of life, "He's making diamonds out of us."[121]

> *I will refine them like silver and test them like gold. They will call on my name and I will answer them; I will say, "They are my people," and they will say, "The Lord is our God."*
> (Zechariah 13:9)

God has not stepped back to let the devil run things for a season, nor is He vindictive. His grace and love do not shield us from the assaults of the world, but He exposes us to them so that in our inadequacies, we cling more tightly to Him.[122] We all recognize that when life is going smoothly, we have little need for help, and our tendency is to be self-sufficient; but when life turns upside-down, we need help. God uses times like these to draw us to Himself, desiring our complete dependence, knowing our needs, better than we do. Our helplessness is actually one of the greatest assets we can have, for when we can do nothing at all, we receive the most spectacular answers to prayer.[123] When we need Jesus, we will find that He is faithful. He will never leave us or forsake us.

Be content with what you have, because God has said,
"Never will I leave you; never will I forsake you."
(Hebrews 13:5)

Some of us regard negative experiences as an indication of our substandard Christian life and wonder where we have failed. We think spiritual maturity should be characterized by unshadowed and trouble-free living.[124] Dietrich Bonhoeffer says "every Christian has his own cross waiting for him, a cross destined and appointed by God. Each must endure his allotted share of suffering and rejection. But each has a different share: some God deems worthy of the highest form of suffering and gives them the grace [even for martyrdom], while others He does not allow to be tempted above that which they are able to bear."[125] The stronger we become spiritually, the more we can handle as we realize God's grace is sufficient and His power is made perfect in our weaknesses (2 Corinthians 12:9). A pastor once told me that if I was not experiencing trials in my life, I should question the depth of my spirituality. Ouch! God exercises us in tougher and tougher schools.[126] In our own inadequacy, we have the joy of seeing God's sufficiency as our problems set the scene for God's glorious intervention,[127] even if it is in us and not the situation. His love, goodness, faithfulness and power are at work in us, perfecting us, even when we don't see or understand His ways.

Consider Joseph (Genesis 37–42). His cruel brothers sold him into Egyptian slavery. That didn't seem like a good plan for Joseph, and certainly caused him a great deal of discomfort, but God eventually used this to save the entire nation of Israel from famine. Many years later Joseph was able to say, "You intended it to harm me, but God intended it for good" (Genesis 50:20). The difficulty we experience may also be the means God is using to accomplish something incredible.

The story of Joseph shows that "Satan not only acts within the sovereign permission of God but also ends up accomplishing the sovereign purposes of God."[128] God's sovereignty is evident in the story of Job too. God allowed unbelievable suffering in Job's life, but He was still in control of Satan's schemes giving permission and setting perimeters (Job 1:12, 2:6). When Job and his friends tried to make sense of all this, they were unsuccessful. God's voice thundered in power when He told Job that He is so much greater than mere men and should not even be questioned (Job 38–41). He will do what He will do. Our understanding or approval is inconsequential. "For my thoughts are not your thoughts, neither are your ways my ways," declares the LORD" (Isaiah 55:8). When it comes right down to it, God's ways are a mystery, impossible to explain away.

> For who is able to resist his will? But who are you, a human
> being, to talk back to God? Shall what is formed say to the
> one who formed it, "Why did you make me like this?"
> (Romans 9:19–20)

Catherine Marshall, whose husband Peter died of cancer, wrote that wisdom and understanding are baits to our own autonomy. If we were to understand it all, we would no longer have need of God, for we would be like Him. The Tree of Knowledge was what tempted Eve. She wanted to be wise, knowing everything. Our need to know "why" is forbidden fruit in direct opposition to faith and trust.[129] As long as we wear the garment of flesh, we can never understand the mind of our Creator, except that which He chooses to reveal to us.[130] J. I. Packer wrote, "For the truth is that God in His wisdom, to make and keep us humble, and to teach us to walk by faith, has hidden from us almost everything that we should like to know about the providential purposes which He is working out in our lives.[131]

The presence and love of God is not measured by how He changes the circumstances or performs miracles. Don't let your need to understand distract you from God's presence.[132] Trust is not a natural response especially for those who have been deeply wounded, but God's Spirit will help us[133] trust Him more and cling to Him in our hour of need. He is especially there in the storms. Nahum 1:3 says that storms are the dust of God's feet. Storms indicate God is moving.

Where was God on April 16, 2007, when Virginia Polytechnic Institute experienced a horrific day of evil? Thirty-two students were shot and killed by a gunman, and an additional seventeen were wounded. Caleb was there, witnessing this tragedy firsthand, experiencing unimaginable grief, and asking this tough question: "Where are you, God?"

Caleb remembers that months before the incident, he was walking on campus with a friend. Both felt that the Holy Spirit was alerting them to God's intent to do something significant in their community. In retrospect, Caleb feels it was not a coincidence that churches began teaching about pain and suffering and that many began praying ardently for the community.

On April 12, at a Campus Crusade meeting, the leaders prayed passionately. This type of prayer increased in fervor as they interceded for those on campus who didn't know Jesus. A few days later, on April 15, though he didn't know why, Caleb remembers asking God to break the heart of this campus as He drew people to Himself. Little did he know that God had put that prayer on his heart because of what was about to happen.

On April 16, the voice of evil made a loud and clear statement. Its message was death, destruction, harm and hatred. It wasn't the only voice heard. God was also speaking in His quiet way. Caleb observed, "He might not have sounded like what we wanted to hear, but He is a great communicator and can speak in ways other than words. He spoke through His Word and whispered comfort into our souls at the most difficult of times."

Two days after this tragedy, parents, students and the Campus Crusade leaders gathered at the freshman-sophomore prayer meeting. Caleb, crying, stood up to help lead worship, focusing on who God is and what He will do. He said that he felt closer to God at that moment than he ever had before. An unexplainable and overwhelming sense of peace and love enveloped him. It could only have come from God in their midst. Caleb said, "I believe God was crying with us."

In the weeks that followed, prayer groups proliferated. Caleb remembers praying more than he ever had before. They stood in circles holding hands, and when they opened their eyes, crowds had gathered, and strangers had joined them. They shared Jesus's love with many different people and had tough discussions about the brevity of life and its meaning.

Months later, Caleb's unanswered questions came to a climax. He needed to hear from God. While hiking in the mountains, he stopped at a secluded spot where a fallen tree was suspended, leaning on its neighbor. There God spoke to him through Zephaniah 3:17 (ICB): "The Lord your God is with you. The mighty One will save you. The Lord will be happy with you. You will rest in his love. He will sing and be joyful about you." Suddenly new life and energy entered his soul. God loved him and was with him. What else did he need to know?[134]

God doesn't always give us the answers we seek, but He will show up, affirming His love, and strengthening and comforting us. Bill told of a time when he was totally devastated. "My father, still a relatively young man and extremely active, died of a heart attack. That night in bed, I wrestled with God. "Why did this happen?" Suddenly, in the middle of the night, everything changed. God simply said, 'I'm able. I'm enough for you. Right now you doubt this, but trust Me.' In the middle of the bleakest night I have ever known, one overpoweringly intimate moment with God gave me courage, reassurance and hope."[135]

Difficulties are the avenue to spiritual maturity. "Eyes washed by tears can see God more clearly."[136] "Troubles almost always makes us look to God, but His blessings tend to divert our attention elsewhere."[137] C. S. Lewis said,

"Pain insists upon being attended to. God whispers to us in our pleasures, speaks in our consciences, but shouts in our pains. It is His megaphone to rouse a deaf world."[138]

One way that God uses difficulties in our lives is to get our attention. Charles Stanley says that He might use blessings and answered prayer, but He also might use unanswered prayer, disappointment, failure, financial collapse, tragedy and illness. Dr. Stanley shared a story of a time when an illness put him flat on his back. He was hospitalized for several weeks. "If someone had prayed for God to heal me, I would have missed one of the greatest spiritual times in my entire life. I needed to hear from God. An illness can be God's way of helping us examine our lives."[139]

Lynne shared this story about her breast cancer diagnosis. In her case, God used her diagnosis to expose sin in her life. She wrote, "Though intellectually I knew I was forgiven and that God loved me, I still struggled with a sense of failure and rejection as I approached my treatment. Somehow, I felt 'less than' as I stood before God. I had asked God for a verse to encourage me and help me get through my surgery, but He had not led me to anything. The morning of my mastectomy, my sister texted me this verse… The words penetrated my heart in a way that nothing else had, and spoke directly to my feelings of rejection. I believe it was the special Scripture I had asked for."

*I said, "You are my servant; I have chosen you and have **not rejected you**. So do not fear, for I am with you; do not be dismayed, for I am your God. I will strengthen you and help you; I will uphold you with my righteous right hand."*
(Isaiah 41:9–10, emphasis added)

God wants us to be dependent on Him. When the problem is so big that we begin to realize our own inability to cope, we are inclined to turn to God.

Fox hole conversions are legendary. Pricilla Shirer says, "Sometimes a pressing or ongoing problem, or a crisis that hits us out of the blue, presents the most conducive environment for us to draw closer to Him than ever. Sometimes we won't listen any other way. And He knows it. There's no such thing as a coincidence with God."[140]

God also uses difficulties to shape us into the person He intends us to be. He changes us from the inside out. God isn't doing something *to* us, but is doing something *in* us.[141] God places battles in front of us so we can learn to fight (Judges 3:1–2). If we need patience, it is developed by frustration. If we need sensitivity or compassion, it is developed by sorrow. Perseverance, trust and faith are nurtured by waiting in dark places. Because He loves us so much, He wants us to become mature and complete, lacking nothing (James 1:4). The only way to get there is through trials and tribulations, orchestrated for our benefit by a loving God. "We can rest confident in the fact that nothing will happen to us in this world apart from the gracious will of a sovereign God. Nothing."[142] If we want to say "God didn't do this" and attribute circumstances to something or someone outside of God's influence, we negate His sovereignty.

"We should not, therefore, be too taken aback when unexpected and upsetting and discouraging things happen to us now. What do they mean? Why, simply that God in His wisdom means to make something of us which we have not attained yet, and is dealing with us accordingly. Perhaps He means to strengthen us in patience, good humour, compassion, humility, or meekness, by giving us some extra practice in exercising these graces under specially difficult conditions. Perhaps He has new lessons in self-denial and self-distrust to teach us. Perhaps He wishes to break us of complacency, or unreality or undetected forms of pride and conceit... Or perhaps God is preparing us for forms of service of which at present we have no inkling. Perhaps His purpose is simply to draw us closer to Himself...for fellowship with the Father and the Son is most vivid and sweet... when the cross is the heaviest. Meanwhile, we ought not to hesitate to trust His wisdom, even when He leaves us in the dark."[143]

When we struggle, we become more sensitive to others who are struggling in the same way. Others are strengthened and inspired by our perseverance. "He comforts us every time we have trouble so that when others have trouble, we can comfort them with the same comfort God gives us" (2 Corinthians 1:4 ERV).

A person who responded to the survey added this insight. "It's usually during the tough times that the channels of communication (to God) are clearest. I've had physical challenges (leukemia) and emotional ones (depression). These times and situations drive me deeper into the Word and prayer. C. S. Lewis's book, *The Problem of Pain,* has ministered to me a great deal. Lewis underscores that it's not God's job to make me happy. It's His job to make me more like His Son. Many times, that chiseling and carving to make me more like Jesus hurts, but that's when I hear God the clearest. The leukemia has given me wide open doors to share His goodness. The depression has made me sensitive to others with the same proclivity and that's when I really understand 2 Corinthians 1 (comfort others with the comfort with which He comforts me)."

Jay Bufton was hospitalized, dying of cancer. His positive attitude, joy and faith were beacons of light to everyone around him. The hospital staff and visitors were drawn to his room. Jay recognized God's hand and said that though this disease harmed him, God was using it for good, allowing him to tell many people about Jesus. His funeral was a testament to his faithful witness and the fact that God had taken something terrible and used it for good.[144]

There are numerous instances of God mightily using what we would consider to be terrible tragedies for remarkable results. Rachel Scott, Joni Erickson Tada and Bethany Hamilton are just a few examples of how God can take an ordinary life and make it extraordinary by subjecting it to misfortune. The result becomes something much greater than could have been possible otherwise.

In whatever difficulties we experience, we have a choice. We can either develop a deep dependence on God or enter into despair.[145] We can fall into a pit of anger and hopelessness, or we can climb the ladder to rise above the problem and begin to see God's perspective.[146] Instead of railing against God and being angry when He doesn't seem to be there, we must seek Him and then submit to Him. When things go wrong, instead of getting so upset, we should try to listen harder for whatever God is trying to tell us.[147] We can even approach the negative times in our life with humor. A friend who was a cancer patient quipped, "I like having cancer because now people have to listen to me." Another friend said that his chemo treatments gave him the opportunity to tell a captive audience of fellow cancer patients about God, and they couldn't get away.

God's reasons for our troubles may only become evident in retrospect, or we may never understand why, yet we can thank Him for His help and strength, His work during the problem, and for His eventual solution. He is working even when we don't see or understand, turning troubles into blessings. Trust in His love and goodness. He knows what He is doing. His way is best, so learn to depend on Him.

Bernadette's story of taking her dying husband, Giff, to hospice moved me deeply. He had been diagnosed with brain cancer, and they prayed for his healing. Eight years later, after enduring surgeries, radiation and chemotherapy, his pain and seizures necessitated moving him to hospice. In the midst of this pain and grief, Bernadette was able to depend on God. She shared this story from her blog.

"Sometimes, *new beginnings* don't start with silver linings, but are forged through trials in our lives. Psalms 23:4 sustained me. 'Yea, though I walk through the valley of the shadow of death, I will fear no evil: for thou art with me; thy rod and thy staff they comfort me.'

In my heart, that cold January morning, the birds weren't singing, the sun wasn't shining. A heavy grey cloud was shadowing over us. That verse kept playing over and over in the fibers of my mind and heart.

Check-in time was just a few hours away. With great reluctance I helped my husband get ready. He was being more resistant than normal. When I asked him why, he said, "Why hurry, when I'm just going there to die?" In my attempt to comfort him, it became harder to hold back the tears. My whole body was crying, yet I felt only numbness on the journey to hospice. Our steps and hearts were weighted, knowing he would not be coming back home.

We placed our trust in the Lord entirely, knowing the outcome. He was allowing us to enter a sacred place of helplessness, into total humility and brokenness to experience His holy grace and mercy. Understandably, neither one of us spoke along the way. The walk we were taking through the valley that day held two different meanings for two different people.

My steps were slow and grieved, not wanting to check him in. With great reluctance, I released him in the care of the warm and compassionate caregivers. My heart quivered with deep grief and sorrow. All I wanted to do was run into the arms of Jesus for my husband's healing and comfort for my troubled heart.

As I walked out the doors that evening, I knew the walk through this valley, would eventually come to a close. I had prayed for healing and would not stop requesting that of God until He gave me an answer.

My husband endured two more months in hospice of failing health, pain and seizures. Many visitors came to offer prayers, smiles and fellowship. Once when a friend came to visit him in his darkened room, he told her God had told him he had two more weeks before going home to be with the Lord.

I moved into hospice to stay with him for the remaining time, though I continued to pray for his healing. Three days before the end of the two weeks, God also told me about the timing, so I could be prepared. He said, 'I am taking Giff in one direction and you in another.' Would I continue to have the faith to fear no evil, for God was with me? Would I continue, as a widow, to seek the comfort of Christ's rod and staff to protect and guide me and my family?

The evening before his death our pastor called to comfort and pray with me. During our prayer time I realized the Lord did answer my prayer. Through my prayers, mountains and obstacles were moved for my own faith and heart to be strengthened and secure in God. Giff went home, peacefully, to be with the Lord the next day in the early morning.

It seems God does His best work in the valley. He understands the cost to us to painstakingly walk into the shadows and darkness. Do we trust God enough? How eager we are to run to receive the blessings from our Father's hand on the mountain top, but in our darkest hours, His light shines anew in our lives. We can trust Him, *even in the valley.*"[148]

When we think about it, the mountain tops in Colorado, though beautiful, are rocky and barren. Yes, the views are spectacular, and we can see a long way. The exhilaration of the accomplished climb invigorates us. But there isn't much growth high on the tundra. Growth happens in the valleys.[149]

Consider it pure joy, my brothers and sisters, whenever you face trials of many kinds, because you know that the testing of your faith produces perseverance. Let perseverance finish its work so that you may be mature and complete, not lacking anything.
(James 1:2–4)

As we grow and mature through God's refining and molding, can we come to the place of accepting the path He has asked us to walk? Can we even embrace it, rejoicing in trouble? Oswald Chambers said that, "No matter how difficult something may be, I must say, 'Lord, I am delighted to obey you in this.' Discovering a new way of manifesting the Son of God should make our heart beat with renewed excitement."[150] Can we welcome the hurdles, aware of

God's work through them to make us more like Jesus? Our steadfastness can develop a "spiritual vitality" in which we willingly do what the trial demands, no matter how much it hurts, as long as it gives God the opportunity to manifest the life of Jesus in us.[151] It helps to realize that this world is not our final dwelling place. Like Paul, we can say, "For to me, to live is Christ and to die is gain" (Philippians 1:21). The road we travel here, whether rough or smooth, is ultimately a road to heaven.[152]

Joy expressed regrets. Two years ago, her husband, Bob, passed away from cancer. They had spent the last months of his life mustering their faith as they prayed desperately for his healing. The whole church joined in, and they sought every possibility as outlined in Scripture: confessing sin, laying on hands, anointing with oil. They wouldn't even consider another outcome, because such would be a chink in their faith. Yet now Joy wishes she had been more attuned to living each moment in God's presence and daily seeking His will. "For me to live is Christ." Perhaps if she had lived this way, Bob's death wouldn't have been such a monstrous disappointment, and she could have better ministered to those who came to visit. She would have been better prepared to accept God's plan and could even rejoice in the "to die is gain" part, knowing that Bob is now with Jesus.

Isaiah 57:1–2 says that the righteous are taken away from this world to be spared from evil. Death is their gift of rest and peace. Although those of us who are left behind grieve because they're gone and we miss them, it is comforting to realize that God hasn't been unfaithful by allowing them to die, but has instead provided a place for them to be free from the trouble of this world.

Can we get to the place where we thank Him for the problem recognizing His work in us and knowing He already has a plan? Thanking Him for His involvement, even when His answers conflict with our desires, brings peace and changes our outlook from one of despair to hope. We are released from resentment and free to watch God work for our good.

God is pure love and He wants the best for us. "Can anything separate us from the love Christ has for us? Can troubles or problems or sufferings? If we have no food or clothes, if we are in danger, or even if death comes—can any of these things separate us from Christ's love?" (Romans 8:35 ICB). When we hold onto the love of God, even when the odds are against us, something extraordinary happens. We become "super-victors"— "more than conquerors through Him who loved us" (Romans 8:37).[153] He is the one who enables us to tackle whatever comes our way with strength, hope and purpose.

Gail shared that she was devastated when she suffered a miscarriage. All those negative feelings of sadness, anger, depression, helplessness and hopelessness flooded her soul. Yet, when she returned home from the hospital, she sensed God's spirit prompting her to praise. "I will extol the Lord *at all times*; His praise will always be on my lips" (Psalm 34:1, emphasis added). She began singing the doxology. A sense of peace and comfort took the place of her despair.

Eight years ago, my husband, Perry, was diagnosed with multiple sclerosis. Of course, we have prayed for healing, but God has not seen fit to do that. We could be angry. We could plead with God or turn away from Him, but there comes a point of acceptance. We look to see how God can teach us and use us in this problem. We experience a deeper dependency on Him. We have a more potent ministry because of this. Can we find joy even in the MS? Can we even thank God for this disease? That's a tall order, not possible by our own strength and will. But it is possible through His work in us. We still pray for healing but are learning to be content that God will provide His best for us, in His time.

Step out in faith and come into God's presence expectantly. He is always there to give us what is needed to tackle any problem. Louie Giglio talks about God's sufficiency in his video *Indescribable*. The God who made the universe is huge. His majesty is mind boggling. He is big enough for any problem and can and does rescue us in miraculous ways from difficulties sometimes. But sometimes

He is just there, helping us through. We may be at the end of our rope and think we can't handle the situation anymore. Our grief may be consuming us like a suffocating weight on our chests. God does not grow tired or weary. He gives strength to the weary and increased power to the weak (Isaiah 40:28–30), giving us the ability for one more breath, one more step, as we lean on Him.[154] Getting to know God by spending time with Him, helps us to see His love, grace, power, strength, majesty and sovereignty, bringing us to a place of trust and peace, even in the tough times. He is our rock. When our feet are placed solidly on Him, instead of being stuck in the mire, (Psalm 40:2) we are free to dance and sing.

> *And this is my prayer: that your love may abound more and*
> *more in knowledge and depth of insight, so that you may be*
> *able to discern what is best and may be pure and blameless*
> *for the day of Christ, filled with the fruit of righteousness that*
> *comes through Jesus Christ—to the glory and praise of God.*
> (Philippians 1:9–12)

——◆ *Stop and Refresh* ◆——

1. Read Isaiah 40:28–29, Isaiah 55:8–9, and Job 38–40:4. Are we able to understand God's ways and purposes or question Him? Why is our need to know "why" dangerous? Have you ever been angry with God? Is that okay?

2. What do you think God's role is in the suffering and difficulties in the world? Why do bad things happen to good people? Does God treat believers differently than unbelievers? Is God involved? Is God sovereign? Is He adequate?

3. Read 2 Corinthians 3:18, Romans 8:28–30, and James 1:2–4. What is God's highest intent for us as believers? Does He want us to be comfortable and successful? Why or why not?

4. What are some ways God uses difficulties and tragedies in our lives? What purpose can they serve?

5. What does Philippians 1:21, "For to me, to live is Christ and to die is gain," mean to you? Is this a possible reaction to suffering?

Chapter Ten

ARE WE THERE YET?

Discerning the voice of God

"Love the LORD your God, listen to his voice,
and hold fast to him. For the LORD is your life."
(Deuteronomy 30:20)

Y ou've learned that God does indeed want a relationship with you because He loves you. You've seen how to clear the channels to God, with His help, so He can speak, and you can listen. The Bible, your guidebook, has helped you learn about God and what you can expect from Him, and what He expects from you. You've gotten to know your destination by spending time with God.

Now, you're almost ready to sightsee—see what God has in store for you, see Him at work, and hear what He has to say to you. We have just a few items of business to attend to while we're traveling so we can make the most of our time.

Perry and I took a trip to Europe. I read about many of the places we intended to visit, heard about them from others and even saw pictures, but none of those things compared with getting to see those places myself. Standing in front of the Eiffel Tower in Paris, walking through beautiful castles and palaces, riding the waterways of Venice in a gondola—all these were incredible, unforgettable experiences. I didn't want to be done. I wanted to keep seeing and doing, and I want to go back for more visits. My appetite for these wonderful places has been awakened.

In our relationship with God, we can hear what our family, our friends, and our pastors say about seeing or hearing God, but that doesn't even come close to experiencing Him ourselves. Make this personal. "I believe God not because my parents told me, not because the church told me, but because I've experienced His goodness and mercy myself."[155]

Don't just seek the experience and not God Himself though. Our experiences are a doorway to Him, not the goal themselves.[156] God will act differently toward each of us, so we shouldn't expect God to treat us like someone else. God will meet each of us in a unique way, telling us what we need to hear when we need to hear it, and showing us what we need to see when we need to see it. Sir Robert Anderson, who was once the head of Scotland Yard, cautions us by saying, "Among Christians it is pestilently evil to make the exceptional experience of some the rule of faith for all. The Word of God is our guide and not the experience of fellow Christians."[157] We shouldn't feel less spiritually adept if God hasn't spoken to us in some sensational way. In fact, seeking sensational signs is considered evil. "You're looking for proof, but you're looking for the wrong kind. All you want is something to titillate your curiosity, satisfy your lust for miracles" (Matthew 12:39 MSG). God wants us to learn to listen, to recognize His voice and become attuned to it throughout our day, even when it is a still, small voice.

How disappointed we would have been on our trip if we had limited ourselves to just one spot to visit. In retrospect, I don't know what I would have chosen—so many points of interest enthralled us from natural beauty to art, history and culture. When we approach God to see what He has in store for us, we also shouldn't limit Him to a single means or method. We need to be attentive to Him everywhere. He will surprise us.

We also can't live in the past, hanging our hat on an encounter with God that happened a while ago. As great as memories are, I'm not satisfied to quit traveling and just look at picture albums or computer slide shows. I want to keep seeing different places and having new experiences. God wants us to keep experiencing Him too, in an ongoing personal, daily relationship in which we walk and talk with Him all the time.

As we align our minds and spirits with God's Spirit, He *will* speak to us. Expect it. Dallas Willard says that one of the greatest harms religious leaders can do to those in their care is to convince them that God isn't going to meet them personally, and that they need the approval and guidance of their leaders in order to interact with God. Instead ministers should be leading people into an understanding of the voice of God and how it works in their lives, so that they are free to experience their own unique spiritual adventure."[158] The next few chapters will examine ways God speaks and give examples of His interaction with us through personal stories.

Before we begin to see God at work, let's set some ground rules and pay attention to some cautions. When we drove in Europe the rules of the road were new to us, so we had to study to know what to do. If we had violated them, we may have disrupted traffic and made some locals angry. We might have gotten a ticket or even caused an accident.

When we seek to hear God, we must also be aware of cautions and be well-informed, so we can avoid mistakes. Some of the most disruptive occurrences in our spiritual lives and churches come when a person or a group erroneously base their actions on something they claim to have heard from God. This can cause horrible massacres like the Branch Davidians or Jonestown, difficult church splits and painful mistakes in our own lives. Prayerfully seeking God's guidance and learning to accurately discern His voice are important spiritual skills we should work to develop. We shouldn't be afraid to listen and hear God ourselves. We should be confident that God will speak to us and use us as conduits for His messages. Blindly following a charismatic leader who claims to have heard the voice of God can start us down a path to disaster.

God is a God of unity and peace. If there is dissention, we must seek Him and wait on Him humbly for direction. Sometimes God will bring us into agreement. At other times it may be all right to go in different directions, as in the case of Paul and Barnabas in Acts 15:36–41. This may serve to further God's kingdom in new ways, so be open to wherever God leads.

Each of us can learn through experience the particular quality, spirit and content of God's voice, but our discernment will not always be infallible. We can learn to discern God's voice as clearly and with as much accuracy as with anyone with whom we have an intimate relationship.[159] Even in our most intimate human relationships, we hear the wrong message, get the wrong impression and misinterpret what has been said. Yet we keep talking and listening. It's that way with God too. We shouldn't be discouraged if we "get it wrong." Though God is infallible, we aren't. God is patient and will redirect us or stop us when we are in error. Make every effort to pay attention and keep listening as accurately as possible.

Learning to Listen

When Perry and I were in graduate school at Wheaton College, we worked on a curriculum called "Active Listening." Although this was directed to families, many of the principles we learned apply to our relationship with God.

The first step was developing an attentive posture. It is difficult to talk to someone when they are slouching and appear bored and distracted. Body language says a lot. We instructed participants to lean slightly forward, sit erect, and not fidget. When we talk to God, we also need to strike an attentive and receptive posture. For some this is standing, kneeling, or even laying prostrate on the floor. Others prefer to raise their hands to heaven and look up, or bow before Him with open hands. These practices replicate the ways people in the Bible prayed. Curled up on the couch, relaxing on pillows, and munching on snacks is not very conducive to effective communication with God. Although God doesn't set legalistic requirements on our prayer posture, praying fervently and seriously, and coming before Him in reverence and awe, promotes better listening.

Active listening also stresses eye contact. This is a way we show we are paying attention to the speaker. Of course, since God is spirit, we cannot see Him, but we can visualize Him in our minds so we are more attentive to who He is. When I see Him "high and lifted up with the train of his robe filling the temple (Isaiah 6), enthroned in majesty and power, I'm better focused, my faith increases, I'm more connected, and my prayers are more meaningful.

As we studied listening, we identified several filters that distort the message we hear. Busyness, preconceived ideas and only hearing part of the message are all things that get in the way of effective communication. We parents may have had times when we were inattentive to our kids. Does this example sound familiar? "Look-it, Mom. Look-it!" a child said enthusiastically. The mom responded with a detached, "uh huh." "But, Mom, you're not look-iting," the youngster complained in disappointment. Is God trying to show us something, but we are not look-iting because we're too busy?

How many times have you been listening to someone talk, using the time to craft your response? You think you already know what they have to say. If we have preconceived ideas about what we think God should be saying, we may not hear what He actually *is* saying. We jump quickly to conclusions. We may be too practical, skeptical or timid to accept God's more surprising messages. We act on what makes sense to us according to our own understanding, but we've not listened.

We know that the Bible is God's Word, so in our efforts to hear from Him, we find verses to back up our own ideas and plans. When we pick verses out of the Bible, not paying attention to the context or even all of Scripture, the message we get can be in error. God's directives always align to the whole of Scripture. I am reminded of the teenager who heard her parent say, "You can't go to the mall..." She became angry. If she had listened to the whole message she would have also heard, "Until your dad gets home so you can take his car." A favorite trick of our communication professors was to give an exam with the instructions to read it through completely before answering. Most of us immediately started writing. The last statement was to ignore all the questions and only write our names on the paper. We were trained to get the whole message before responding.

The final step in active listening is checking what we thought we'd heard for clarification by repeating the message back to the speaker—getting feedback. We can do this in our relationship to God too, by asking God for clarification. It's helpful to write in a journal and ponder the message. God will often accommodate us by speaking to us in different ways from different sources to make sure we hear Him. Beth Moore wrote, "I know God is speaking to me about a certain matter when it seems like everything I hear or read for a while points toward the same issue."[160]

Our Very Own Guide

When Perry and I were in Florence, Italy, we were thrilled to see Michelangelo's famous statue of David. Our guide informed us that the figure we saw standing in the Piazza della Signoria was not the real McCoy. It was a replica. The real statue had been moved inside the Academia Gallery to protect it from the elements and vandalism. The original had been attacked with a hammer! We wouldn't have known this without the help of our guide.

So, how do we discern what is God's voice and what is not? Thankfully, we also have a guide—the Holy Spirit who lives in us. Part of His job is to convict us of sin and lead us into truth. Lots of people have told me they've had a tugging in their heart, an idea that pops into their heads, or an urge to do something. This may be the Holy Spirit. God's voice is authoritative but not bullying; warm, but firm; quiet, but powerful; divine, but personal. We know the color blue, the taste of a peach, the sound of birds and the smell of a rose because we have been taught about them as children and have experienced these things many times. Recognizing God's voice is similar. We learn, we experience, we practice.[161] Wine connoisseurs have exquisitely developed their ability to taste wines, so much so that they can not only identify the type of wine, but also the vintage as well. As we hone our listening skills, we can become superbly adept at hearing what God is saying. When we identify that voice, we can make the effort to be obedient to what God is asking: talk to that person, make that call, get up and pray, or do whatever He directs. Here are some stories that illustrate the quiet work of the Holy Spirit in the lives of believers.

Chris shared a story about the Holy Spirit's prompting, waking her from a sound sleep to pray.

"I woke up suddenly and glanced at the clock. 3:00 a.m. 'Really? You want me to do what, Lord?' I had the strong impression that I needed to get up and pray for my daughter, Tamara, who lives in another state. I knew she was driving home from a trip, but I didn't know what was wrong. I paced the floor in my robe and slippers, praying for her protection, help or whatever was needed.

The next morning, I called Tamara. Excitedly she told me her story. Her car had a flat tire in the middle of the night on a dark, deserted stretch of road. I had told her never to get out of her car or accept help from strangers. A white van pulled up behind her and two women got out and approached her car. She cracked her window to speak with them. They told her their husbands were back in the van and would like to help her change the tire, but they understood her hesitation. That is why they, the women, had approached her, instead of the men. They would want some kind people to help their daughter if she were in trouble. Tamara agreed to let them help, and the men changed the tire. They followed her to the next town, where unbelievably a service station was still open and had the tire she needed to replace the spare. One of the women gave her a card with their phone number hand-written on it. 'You call us if you need any help. We hope you get home safely.'

Tamara later tried to call the number to thank these couples for their help. The phone was disconnected. After several attempts, she contacted the phone company to check on the number. She was told that the number had never been assigned. But, it had been hand written by the woman. Had she written the wrong number in error? Tamara doesn't think so. She thinks these people were angels, sent by God in answer to her Mom's prayers."

Matt listened to the Holy Spirit when He spoke in the ordinary circumstances of his life. The Power Ball total was in the nine-figure range. People, with eyes set on fast fortune, were buying tickets in bundles. Matt has usually purchased lottery tickets each week, even when the lure was not as significant. When he stopped for gas, he intended to buy his customary ticket. But, this time, he seemed to hear God speak. "If you purchase this lottery ticket, you will win, but it will have a negative impact on you and your family." He decided not to buy the ticket. The security of his family and being obedient to God's voice were more important to him than the lure of wealth.

A survey respondent wrote this story. "One night I was driving on the highway and I felt a strong prompting from the Spirit to change to the far-right lane—slow lane—from the middle lane on a three lane highway. Feeling a bit silly, I thought, 'why not?' I was singing to the radio at the top of my lungs, enjoying the ride, when suddenly I saw a large deer standing in that middle lane where I had been traveling. I switched off the radio and prayed a prayer of thanks for the rest of the ride home.

Another survey responder wrote of his experiences with the Holy Spirit's leading. "I was commuting in heavy traffic on I-95. There was *always* road construction. My attention was drawn to a crane working on a bridge. I felt strongly that I should pray for the workers, so I did. I later saw a story in the newspaper about the crane partially falling through that bridge. The article went on to say that no one was hurt. Everyone was amazed. That's my God!"

Learning to Discern the Voice of God

When my kids or my husband call me on the phone, I recognize their voices immediately. Other people, whom I don't know as well, may have to identify themselves. As we mature in our faith, we will be more able to recognize God voice with accuracy because we know Him. Here are some checks to help us better discern.

The Bible

The Bible is our measuring stick for God's message. This is the primary way God will speak to us. He will not direct us to do anything that is contrary to His Word. People use "God's voice" to rationalize their sin and disobedience, or their own selfish motives. God will not tell someone to cheat on their spouse to show love to that other person, act in revenge towards someone because they deserve to be put in their place, or falsify income tax returns so there is more money to tithe. We can be assured that this is not God speaking, but in fact may be the devil's duping. Pay attention to the whole message of the Bible, not a verse out of context: "Take life easy; eat, drink and be merry." is in the Bible, but it's not very wise counsel (Luke 12:19). The follow-on verse is, "But God said to him, 'You fool! This very night your life will be demanded from you.'" (Luke 12:20).

The Motive

Another discerning check for God's voice is determining our motive. We should ask God to search our hearts to see if there is any wicked way in us. (Psalm 139:23–24) If what we are about to do is for ourselves, and not God's glory, we know it's not Him talking. When celebrities assert that they've heard from God, are they jumping on the current bandwagon to affect public opinion, or sharing their legitimate interaction with God? Skeptics raise an eyebrow, while others celebrate their spiritual attentiveness. We cannot judge. Pastor Jesse Duplantis said God told him to pray for a fifty-four-million-dollar private jet (his fourth private jet) so he could quickly get anywhere in the world with no stops, to share the gospel. He says, "The Lord said, 'I didn't ask you to pay for it, I asked you to believe for it.'"[162] Is this for God's glory or personal notoriety and greed? People have told me they feel directed to invest in a certain stock, buy a fancy house or car, or go somewhere on a trip. Most of the time this kind of inner voice is their own desire, not God's. Carefully consider whether God or the person involved is the focus, and who will receive the glory. If it is the latter, and God is saying "no," we shouldn't stubbornly believe or proceed.

The Risk Factor

God's directives are often risky and "out of the box." When we tackle something that is seemingly impossible, that doesn't particularly make sense, or that causes us to "leave the crowd," we will see the magnitude of God's work and power. Just because the message doesn't seem safe or logical, doesn't mean it isn't from God. Check it out carefully but be willing to take a risk. Be willing to say yes to the ways God is working in your life. Don't bemoan the loss of your comfort but accept the challenge of something new.[163] We needn't fear if God is with us. Be strong and courageous (Joshua 1:9).

Allan was willing to step out in faith and take a risk. In early 2006, he felt God leading him to ask questions about their pastor and his father, the former pastor. It was very difficult time, and people didn't appreciate the interference. Allan was regarded as the evildoer of the church and lost his best friend (associate pastor). He caused stress for the pastor and his wife. Allan's wife begged him to stop before more damage was done. However, he felt that God was prodding him to continue. Finally, reluctantly, the church's trustee board did an audit following the church's seventy-two hour prayer vigil. It was discovered that this pastor and his father were stealing millions of dollars from the church. In just five years, they had stolen three million dollars! The pastor ended up resigning and going to jail. A new pastor came in and the church grew rapidly. The church recently sold their building and purchased a much larger church, and now God is blessing their ministries.

Peace

When we are in tune to God's voice, we will have peace—a supernatural peace that is beyond our understanding. If you feel unsettled, stop. Get back on your knees. Ask God for confirmation in other ways. Ask His spirit to give you peace. Seek Him, allow Him time to speak and be watching. Jesus says, "Peace I leave with you; my peace I give you. I do not give to you as the world gives" (John 14:27). The Holy Spirit provides peace about decisions, but also gives us peace in times of trouble, when we feel unsettled, fearful and upset. We can be assured this supernatural peace is from God.

Several of the responses I've received tell how God gave a sense of peace in the middle of a difficulty.

April shared her story about a time when she was hospitalized with pancreatitis. She was in a great deal of pain and couldn't sleep. About 3:00 a.m. each night, she had explosive vomiting. After ten days, she'd had enough. She told God, "Please heal me or let me die." The next night, at 3:00 a.m., there was silence. She didn't vomit. The light changed to a soft, fuzzy glow and an unimaginable peace descended. Her pain left. She was on the road to recovery.

Johnna told me about a time while she was in seminary, that she was sitting outside on the grass wrestling with some faith questions. Her older sister had been abused by their father, and Johnna was angry. "Where were you, God, when my sister was being abused?" She cried out to God, desperate for an answer. Deep within her spirit, she sensed the Holy Spirit speaking. "I was there. I was crying with her." Johnna said that experience brought her a deep sense of peace as she understood God is always there. This moved her another step closer to forgiving her father.

In their first year of marriage, Annette and David discovered that their unborn child had a sizable tumor. Annette was confined to the maternal/fetal intensive care unit for eight weeks, awaiting the birth. She was scared, wondering if her child would die, and if this would be her only child. One night, around two in the morning, as she lay in bed, she kept hearing someone calling her name. The beds beside her were empty, and the nurses' station was in the far corner of the room. She climbed quietly out of bed, which was no easy feat because she was huge with polyhydramnios (too much amniotic fluid), and started to walk across the room. There was no one around. Now she knew the voice was God. She crawled back in bed, pulled the blankets up under her chin, and listened attentively. A voice spoke into her right ear, "I will never, never leave you." From that point on, her fear was gone and she was confident in God. God gave her immense peace. Her baby was born, survived, and is now a beautiful young woman.

The Community of Believers

It is important for us as believers to be connected with other believers in a small group or other types of close relationships. Our larger church bodies (churches) provide opportunities to hear God's Word, worship, and serve as a "Body of Christ," but it is important to connect in a more intimate way with other believers who can support, encourage and motivate us in our relationship to God. We are not meant to do faith all by ourselves. Hebrews 10:25 encourages us to not give up meeting together. These folks can become our mentors, our prayer partners and our sounding boards, and provide a safe place for us to explore what we believe. "Plans fail for lack of counsel, but with many advisors they succeed" (Proverbs 15:22). Our fellow believers can help us discern what God is saying.

A friend shared her story about how important her "community of believers" has become in her and her husband's lives. Circumstances dictated their move to the Denver area. They had struggled to find time for God, and most of the time, didn't even want to spend time with Him. God was calling. In their new neighborhood, they were invited to a Bible study group. Their eyes, ears and hearts were opened, and they developed a desire to have a deeper relationship with their Lord and Savior. Years and years later, they have found this family of believers to be their special family. They've received many opportunities to serve together. They now praise God that He put them in this place where they could grow and thrive.

The Fleece

Gideon was intimidated by God's directive to him. God wanted him, a simple farmer, to lead the nation of Israel into battle with very few resources. "God, are you sure?" Gideon asked. He "put out fleeces" twice, asking God to either make the fleece wet with dew and the ground dry, or vice versa (Judges 6:36–40). This was a way God verified the plan, and in his certainty, Gideon could be obedient. We can also use this method to verify God's voice.

A survey response contained this story about a fleece. "I was considering taking a sabbatical for a year and laid out three fleeces knowing it would be impossible for them to happen. All three came about. Not only did I take the year off, but I later learned that my children and grandchildren would be in the country for six months. I had extra time to spend with them. In addition, I ended up having to care for my in-laws. God knew I needed this time, and even before I prayed, God provided."

Test the Spirits

"Do not believe every spirit but test the spirits to see whether they are from God, because many false prophets have gone out into the world. This is how you can recognize the Spirit of God: Every spirit that acknowledges that Jesus Christ has come in the flesh is from God, but every spirit that does not acknowledge Jesus is not from God." (I John 4:1–3) Jesus is preeminent. Whatever is happening should bring honor and glory to Him, not ourselves or another. One of the gifts of the Holy Spirit is discernment. "The person without the Spirit does not accept the things that come from the Spirit of God but considers them foolishness and cannot understand them because they are discerned only through the Spirit" (1 Corinthians 2:14).

Our small group of believers has experienced what it is like to come face to face with evil forces. We've learned that they are very real. We had been discussing some experiences of encountering evil spirits and when we started to pray, we felt an oppressive presence. The light seemed to dim and the air became heavy. We immediately began asking Jesus to intervene because "He who is in you is greater than he who is in the world" (1John 4:4). When we prayed, the sensation dissipated. We can ask God to give us a sensitivity to the spirit world, so that we will sense when something is amiss, and then call on Jesus's power to intervene, thwarting the activity of evil.

The Results

Many times we will see God's hand in retrospect, and realize He indeed has been speaking through our circumstances. However, the result isn't always an indicator of whether or not we have accurately followed God's directions. The Old Testament prophets were called by God to get the people of Israel to repent. They suffered greatly for delivering this message, and were unsuccessful in convincing them to turn from their evil ways. The apostles were faithful in following God's commands, yet were beaten, imprisoned and exiled, eventually put to death. Even Jesus, who perfectly had the mind of God, offended people by his words and deeds and was crucified.

Several of our survey responders told stories of times when they thought they had followed God's will, but it turned out badly. They confronted people about sinful practices, spoke out about injustices and presented the gospel. The results were sometimes disastrous. Relationships were ruined and financial difficulties ensued. They were left to wonder if God had really called them.

My neighbor and I were close friends. Although she was curious about my relationship to God, she preferred her own way. One afternoon, she visited a fortuneteller who told her she would be married again. She understood this to mean she should divorce her husband, so she told him that was what she planned to do. He was devastated. She began "dating," even while married, and had men spend the night at her house while her husband still lived there. Some of these men were involved in drugs and other illegal practices.

I could hardly stand to watch her destroy her life and marriage, so I invited her to lunch. I confronted her about her poor choices. I gave her a Bible with highlighted salvation passages, placed in a first aid box. I told her that when she eventually realized she had not chosen the right path, this would help her get back on track.

She was offended and stormed out of the restaurant. Later, one of her boyfriends threatened me with a gun because I had hurt her feelings. I had to call the police. She never spoke to me again. She moved away, and the last thing I heard was that she was traveling in Europe with one of her beaus.

I have often wondered, "Did I do the right thing?" Was I acting zealously on my own initiative (Romans 10:2)? Did I fail to wait for God's timing? If I bungled this, I can only pray that God will take the words and plant them in her life so that at some point she will remember them, and seek God, turning from her destructive choices.

If things go wrong when we thought we heard God speak, evaluate. Did we hear God, or was it our own voice? Were our motives pure, or were we acting out of selfish desires? Did we run ahead with our own timing, or did we wait on God? Even if we have the best of intentions and are trying to represent Him well, we must wait on Him, finding out what He is doing, and joining Him, rather than taking off on our own and asking Him to join us. I have learned that it is the Holy Spirit who brings light, convicts of sin and draws people to God, so my best arguments and most eloquent words will be fruitless without the Holy Spirit's leading. "The Father is the one who sent me, and he is the one who brings people to me. I will raise them up on the last day. Anyone the Father does not bring to me cannot come to me" (John 6:44 ERV).

We shouldn't feel we've failed and give up if things don't work out as we'd hoped. Continue to look for God in the situation. It may take years for Him to act. All He asks is that we are faithful to His voice.

It is the spirit in a person, the breath of
the Almighty, that gives them understanding.
(Job 32:8)

——•♦ *Stop and Refresh* ♦•——

1. Why is it important to experience God yourself and not pattern your experiences after someone else's?

2. Read Matthew 12:38–39. We want to hear from God, so why is it considered evil to seek sensational signs from Him?

3. How can we apply the principles of "active listening" in our relationship with God? Have you had an experience where you heard the Holy Spirit's still, small voice? What happened? What do we do if things turn out poorly?

4. Situation ethics, in which people believe they should do whatever a situation dictates, is a popular persuasion. Are there absolutes? Would God ever direct us to do something that was contrary to Scripture, even if it was for good? Why or why not?

5. What are some ways we can discern whether or not we have heard God's voice? If we are in a good relationship with God, will we always be accurate? Why is it important to be connected to a community of believers?

Chapter Eleven

WE'VE ONLY JUST BEGUN

God's calling

"Trust in the Lord with all your heart,
And lean not on your own understanding
In all your ways acknowledge Him,
And He shall direct your paths.
(Proverbs 3:5–6 NKJV)

Y ou made it! God has so much in store for you. As you journey with Him and see what He has to show you, He will work in and through your life, doing incredible, surprising things. Elisabeth Elliot reminds us that the recognition of who God is and how He works, is a life-long process.[164] You have lots to see!

Our survey showed that people are most interested in receiving guidance from God—more so than any other request of Him. We want to know whether or not we are in God's will, what we should be doing, and what decisions we should make. God is faithful in responding to these prayers, but many times we still find ourselves in a quandary, wishing for clearer information. The next two chapters will help you notice ways God might speak to you, direct you and call you into His service. The stories illustrate ways He has worked in the lives of others so you can be more aware of how God might work in your life.

"How do I know that he's the one?" one of the survey responders asked God about her boyfriend. As she was thinking about this, she turned to get clothes out of her closet and a heard a voice, clear but quiet, that said, "Patience." She immediately knew it was God, and she felt an overwhelming sense of peace. The situation turned out for the best in answer to her prayer.

God sometimes surprises us with His directions, though. We might not even be looking when we hear from Him, yet He speaks unmistakably into our lives.

Caroline wrote that she woke up one night at 2:00 a.m. and suddenly said, "I want to finish my book." Where did that come from so abruptly? Several years earlier, she had begun a book about being an abused Christian woman, but when she remarried and had children, it was put away for "someday." Finishing it was neither on her mind nor her desire.

Caroline said she recognized that this was from God. She had learned not to ignore Him when He speaks to her. She had a job with Community Bible Study and was a wife and mother of seven. Under these circumstances, writing a book was impossible. She discussed this with God and by 4:00 a.m. had decided she needed to quit her job at CBC, which she loved. Once the decision was made, God took away her desire for CBC and replaced it with a passion for abused women. It took her four years, but she published her book, and then another book two years later. She has helped people all over the world through what she's written in her books, on Facebook and on her blog. She eventually went back to school to get a degree in counseling and is now a paid counselor working primarily with abuse victims.

Rebecca was surprised when God spoke to her about going back to school. She said He spoke so clearly in her mind that He may as well have written it in the sky. He said, "It is time for you to go back to school and get your teaching certificate." The rest of the day was like a video playing in her mind where God walked her through all the reasons that this made sense. She had thought about this before, so the idea wasn't totally unprecedented, but it caught her off guard nonetheless. She did follow His request and eventually got her Master of Education and taught in their Catholic school for ten years. She feels so blessed that God encouraged her to follow His plan for her.

A young man shared a story of a time when he was commuting between graduate school and work. He was having a conversation with himself about how he would apply the day's lesson to ministry if he were a pastor. Suddenly, he heard a voice in his mind saying, "You will be a pastor in a rural church." After years of confusion about where his life was headed, and why he was in graduate school, he finally understood and had a sense of peace.

Scott's wife and child had been killed in an automobile accident. The idea of remarrying was far from his mind. Completely out of the blue God said to him, "Scott, you have my permission to remarry." That was a sign to him that he could keep his eyes open. A year and a half later, after his special word from God, he wed Rose and has now been married to her for forty-two years.

Sometimes God speaks in a dramatic way, telling us just where He wants us, in no uncertain terms. Kent experienced this one morning as he got in his car to drive to work as an accountant for a car dealership. The radio was usually on, but this morning it was silent. There seemed to be someone in the car with him. He looked to the passenger seat but saw no one there. He figured he was just stressed and dismissed the sensation. A few minutes later, the invisible companion spoke. I have a job for you and I want you to take it. Then the presence was gone. Kent thought it would be a different job opportunity. He was glad the radio was off, because he's not sure he would have heard the voice otherwise.

Two days later, the encounter nearly forgotten in the midst of his busyness, Kent was asked to volunteer at a church as their treasurer. He knew immediately this was something he was supposed to do, though he was still busy with the demands of his current job. Years later, he applied for a position as a financial administrator of a different church. His volunteer work had prepared him for the new responsibilities. Though he took a significant pay cut, and his current employer tried to dissuade him by offering lucrative incentives, Kent believed God called him to work at the church. He recently retired after seventeen years on the job. He says that this was a good move for him, and he feels blessed to have worked in a job that was so definitely God's calling.

God's guidance isn't always telling us what to do. God may also keep us from making decisions or doing something that isn't in our best interest.

Chuck, a young forester, lost his job. His wife was pregnant with twins. He looked and looked but couldn't find work. In desperation, he called out to a God he didn't know. Several weeks later, he finally did get a job with the Colorado State Forest Service, requiring a move to Golden, Colorado. His new boss was a Christ-follower who led a weekly Bible study for his employees. Chuck began to attend, and he soon believed in Jesus too.

Chuck became passionate about God's Word. He had known nothing about it, so he devoured it with an insatiable hunger. He was dissatisfied with his current job, however and began hunting for new opportunities. A friend had an idea. "Let's open a sawmill together." They identified and obtained permission to manage a large area of land that would provide a supply of timber for a number of years. Chuck was excited about the prospect and began to pray about it. During one of his early morning prayer sessions, he heard a loud voice with a resounding "NO! STOP IT!" He sat up straight in his chair, surprised and amazed at the voice. As he quieted down, he realized this was God. In quieter, loving tones, now in his mind, God continued to assure him that He would take care of him and his family. He was told he needed to appreciate the gift of work that had been provided in answer to his earlier prayers when he was unemployed, and learn to be content.

Now, many years later, after thirty-five years with the Forest Service, Chuck continues to work in forestry. God has indeed provided for all his needs and taken care of him and his family. Chuck is grateful for God's unquestionable direction.

Karen was working at a school-based inner-city clinic for teens. God very clearly told her *not* to do something. Here is her story.

"Our administration had just approved Plan B Birth Control, to be dispensed at our clinic. I had heard debates regarding this 'emergency contraception.' I wanted to learn more about it to be informed, so I took a sample off the shelf to read the insert. I immediately felt something like a bolt of lightning course through my body. It was so forceful that I fell back and dropped the box. I was terrified because I had never had anything like that happen before.

It shook me up all day, and needless to say, I didn't go near those samples again. When I went home, I discussed it with my husband, and he recognized this as the Holy Spirit. We prayed about it and I felt peace. In my remaining time at the clinic, I never prescribed 'Plan B,' and was able, with God's help, to bring a very successful faith-based abstinence/pregnancy program into the school."

God doesn't always speak in words or dramatic ways. He works in our lives to orchestrate circumstances and opportunities, opening and closing doors as He gently leads us to where we need to be. My friend Ed shared several stories about how God has worked in his life, always leading him to the right place where he could have a special ministry, make an impact, or learn an important skill.

Ed and his wife accepted a three-year assignment in Australia to do weather research, seeding clouds to increase rainfall. On clear days, with extra time on his hands, he began reading. A road he frequently traveled passed the headquarters of the Christian Literature Crusade, so he stopped by and selected books to read. The staff encouraged him to start a ministry in outback towns, supplying literature to churches. Since the program was so successful, a Lutheran pastor requested that a truckload of literature from a different national bookstore be delivered. Not only did this ministry create a hunger among the people for Christian literature, but a discouraged Anglican priest was energized to provide an enthusiastic ministry for his small congregation. Ed himself discovered "Evangelism Explosion" (EE) in the literature he read, and this became a passion of his.

While Ed's assignment in Australia was coming to an end, he began job hunting. He received an unsolicited letter from the World Meteorological Organization, inviting him to apply for a job in Cyprus setting up a cloud seeding program. He was chosen and accepted the position, though he had a strange sadness about his choice. He later learned it was only a six-month assignment and he needed long-term employment because he and his wife were starting a family. He was especially disappointed when another job became available in Hawaii. He believed he should honor his commitment to Cyprus, however. Two days before they were to leave, Turkey invaded Cyprus. The job was canceled. This, he believes, was the cause of the sadness he had experienced.

Now Ed was unemployed. He had a wife and new baby in his care. Nothing came of his numerous letters and inquiries. He went to a national weather conference in Florida and was surprisingly notified that he had been accepted for a position in Miles City, Montana. He hadn't even applied for it. He also had an opportunity while he was at the conference to receive intense training in the Evangelism Explosion curriculum at the church in Florida where the program had started. This was the inspiration he needed to continue with EE.

God had Ed's whole path planned, beginning with his reading in Australia. Since he hadn't taken the job in Hawaii, and the job in Cyprus was canceled, Ed was available for the position in Montana. The local church had been trying to use the Evangelism Explosion program with minimal success. There was a lack of leadership. They had been praying for someone from the outside to come and jumpstart their program. God sent Ed. Ed says, "God was directing many things in my life to bring me to that remote area of Montana in answer to the prayers of a congregation." Incredibly, a year later, a letter arrived at his home in Montana, that had been mailed to his address in Australia by his future boss, asking him to apply for the Montana job. It had been lost in the mail. Another contact had initiated Ed's application, so he had been accepted without ever seeing that letter.

It is remarkable how God directs us, sometimes without us even being aware. That is why it is so important to trust Him, even when disappointing things happen like Ed's Cyprus experience. I've researched how God has called and directed people and have been amazed and inspired by the many ways God works, often without speaking. Nevertheless, He is communicating His intent.

I sat surrounded by the plump cushions of an easy chair, sipping my hot cup of coffee. Across from me sat Pastor John Martz, also drinking his steamy brew. We had met at a coffee shop to discuss hearing God. "I've never heard God speak," Pastor John said, and I drew a sharp breath. Really? He had been in ministry for over thirty years and was now retired, but he had never heard God speak?

I asked him how he had been called into ministry. He told me that as an eighth grader, some young men challenged him to get more serious about his spiritual life. As he began to do so, he developed a passion for studying God's Word and found he liked to preach—and was good at it. This was confirmed by others. Becoming a pastor seemed a logical choice.

Peter Marshall, a renowned man of God and chaplain of the U.S. Senate, also said he did not hear God speak, but it was evident in his life that God was leading, redirecting him from ministries in Scotland and China to the United States. His direction came through providential circumstances plus a strong inner feeling of rightness about a particular decision. Doors opened and closed, placing him just where God wanted him to be.[165]

Other pastors told me similar stories about their "calling" to ministry. Corey had struggled with depression in high school and the resulting counseling developed a passion in his soul to help people. He first became a youth pastor, then a lead pastor.

Nate sat in a mission's conference with his dad. As the speakers talked about serving God, he felt a tug in his heart, and made a silent commitment. He didn't become a missionary. Circumstances dictated seminary and becoming an associate pastor instead.

Pastor Wes says that his call to Christian ministry was not hearing an audible voice of God, but a growing internal conviction and a deep desire to share the gospel. He described it as "a fire in his soul that he could not shake off or keep to himself." In addition, he received confirmation from other Christians and church leaders who affirmed the call and his giftedness for preaching.[166]

You may be getting the picture here. God doesn't always speak in words. In fact, His actions may speak louder than His words. Many people, like Pastor John, have told me that they haven't heard God speak, but it is evident in their lives that they are communicating with Him. God can guide us like we guide a car—not speaking but moving us forward with our conscious cooperation.[167]

Sometimes, however, God dramatically intervenes to change the intended course of our lives. We see this happening over and over again in Bible stories. Moses, Gideon and David, to name just a few Old Testament heroes, did not expect to be doing what God called them to do. In the New Testament, the disciples and Paul probably never thought they would be leaving their ordinary vocations to preach the story of Jesus. An encounter with Jesus was enough to change the course of their lives. This happens today too.

Ron headed off to college on a basketball scholarship. His passion for sports directed him toward a major in physical education. When he found Jesus and became a Christian, he began volunteering at a local church. He was fond of the youth and was asked to speak to them on several occasions. He was good at it. A mentor suggested he consider Christian ministry as a vocation. After consideration and prayer, he changed his college plans and went to seminary. Now, after more than forty years, he is still in the role of a pastor, though his specific ministries have changed over the years. Earlier, he would've never thought of becoming a pastor.

Zach had always dreamed of being a policeman. After graduation from high school, he went to college and majored in political science. He then took the exams to enter the police academy, passing with flying colors. He was to start in a week. His results came back on a Monday, but instead of being happy, he was uneasy. Something was not right. He told no one of his struggle, believing they would think he was misguided, and try to persuade him otherwise. The feeling remained so strong, that by Thursday he called the police headquarters and told them he was no longer interested. You can imagine the reaction of his family, friends and coworkers.

Over the next few years, he worked part-time at a church in production and administration. He struggled with determining what he should be doing. His call was unclear. Eventually, the church needed a youth pastor and asked Zach to step in temporarily. He loved it and asked to stay. Two years into youth ministry he began to feel that he should be better prepared and took Master of Divinity courses online. Upon receiving his degree, he realized that some sort of ministry would be his vocation for the rest of his life. Although he did not hear a direct call from God in words, the urging, the feelings, the restlessness and the circumstances dramatically led him in a different direction than the one he had envisioned for himself.

Circumstances, opened and closed doors, problems, restlessness, an inner passion and giftedness are all ways God communicates with us and points us in the right direction—His direction. Sometimes, like Ed, we don't even notice His work until we look back in retrospect and see how He has orchestrated events in our lives to bring us to the place where He wanted us to be. When we pay attention, and look for God, we will begin to see His hand everywhere, and "hear" what He is asking us to do. The following stories indicate different ways God has called people to follow His plans.

Circumstances

Diana shared a story about God calling her and her husband to ministry in the Ukraine through circumstance and opportunity. She and Gene were retired from their careers—Gene with the Federal Aviation Administration, and Diana as a nurse. Diana had always had a heart for missions, but circumstances moved her elsewhere. Out of the blue, a door opened. Would they be interested in joining a team with Campus Crusade to teach morality and ethics in Ukraine? They began to seek God's will. The first three "check boxes" were accomplished: the opportunity, their agreement as a couple and the desire in their hearts. But now they needed God's provision to move forward. Finances, a language barrier, training, and housing all posed challenges. One by one, God met these challenges and they were on their way. When God calls us, He will not only give us the opportunity, unity of spirit with others involved, and the desire, but He will provide for our needs.

Chad went to college to play baseball. He had no idea what he should choose as a major. His dad pressured him to find something that would be prestigious and provide a good income. Dad would make comments like. "I met someone in pharmaceuticals and they make good money" or, "You're a smart kid. You could be a doctor." Chad tried a few possibilities of majors but wasn't impressed.

After his sophomore year, he went home for the summer and played baseball. He was asked to fill in as a supervisor for a camp—so many kids had shown up that they just needed extra adult bodies. Chad continued to work there, becoming a camp counselor. He loved it. As he and his dad drove back to school after the summer, his dad asked him about his camp counseling experience, and Chad enthusiastically told him he had loved it. Chad was blown away when his dad suggested that he look at a career in youth ministry. This was totally out of character for him. When his dad even contacted the youth pastor at his home church to set up an internship, Chad was more than surprised. He began to pursue this course of study and became a youth pastor. God used both circumstances and his dad's words to redirect him.

Kurt believes that God orchestrates our lives and opens the doors where He wants us to walk and closes those that are not in His plan. If He gives us a green light, go! If it is a red light, stop and reevaluate.

Kurt's scheduled high school was overcrowded. They were planning to go on split sessions, so Kurt would be going to school until six in the evening. Soccer practice made this impossible. As he weighed the alternatives, he decided to enroll in a Christian high school. He had a few friends that attended there.

Spirituality was not a priority of his, so he doesn't feel that his faith grew very much even in a Christian high school. What he does value is all the biblical and theological knowledge he received. God was setting the stage.

Later, while in college, Kurt went to a youth group where he received more sound biblical training. Once, the group went to see the movie *The Passion of the Christ*. He was deeply impacted by the message and realized he needed to pursue a deeper relationship with Jesus, using the knowledge he had received. He wasn't sure how this would happen exactly, but he was open to possibilities.

At school, he was taking education classes, interspersed with ministry classes, thinking he would be a teacher. The education classes were boring, but he liked his youth ministry classes. As part of the youth ministry program he had to do a church internship. It was so much fun. He thought, "How cool it would be to do something that was so much fun for a career!"

Kurt is now a youth pastor, impacting kids' lives and relating well to their struggles. As he looks back, he notes that God never spoke to him, but he sees the amazing ways God orchestrated opportunities, people, and even a movie to place him where he needed to be.

Restlessness

Another way God speaks to us is through our restlessness and uneasiness. We might feel like there should be something else, something more, and we begin looking, open to possibilities. Like Zach, it will sometimes take a great deal of courage to restructure our lives, especially when others think we're foolish.

Jordan, a new pastor, said he had graduated from college and started a business. He was restless. Eventually he sought counseling to get his life on track. These sessions developed his own interest in counseling and he went back to school to get a counseling degree, leaving his business. Doors opened. Doors closed. He found himself in the role of an associate pastor—a job which he now pursues with passion.

Restlessness, however can come from our own lack of contentment, not from God, so it is important to discern here. Any work, big or small, notable or obscure, is a blessing. King Solomon said that work is a gift from God (Ecclesiastes 3:13) and we should be grateful for what He has given us to do.

> *A person can do nothing better than to eat and drink and find*
> *satisfaction in their own toil. This too, I see, is from the hand of*
> *God, for without him, who can eat or find enjoyment?*
> (Ecclesiastes 2:24–25)

Being appreciative of all our tasks, important or mundane, gives us a new perspective. "Whatever your hand finds to do, do it with all your might, not to please men, but to please God" (Ecclesiastes 9:10; Galatians 1:10). Like Paul, we can learn to be content and thankful in all sorts of circumstances. (Philippians 4: 11–13) If you are restless, seek God. Is your restlessness an impetus from God to get going and move on, or is it from your own disgruntled spirit? As you seek and submit to Him, God will show you His plan and give you peace and direction.

Al was a new Army lieutenant on his way to the First Battalion (reinforced), Third Infantry Regiment (The Old Guard), at Fort Myer, Virginia. Here are his comments about this assignment, which was not something he wanted.

"I had never heard of The Old Guard, but when I found that it was (in my sophomoric view) a prissy-pants outfit that did nothing but look pretty, I was not happy. This was not the place for the Army's newest version of George Patton. My letter to the Army's Personnel Center (MILPERCEN) explaining this erroneous assignment came back with a terse but clear response. So I reported to Fort Myer, but mentally fought the duty and had a visibly negative attitude for about a month.

Finally one morning, God got my attention. Driving in to work and mentally grousing about a great combat-type infantryman being forced to focus on spit-shined shoes and thumb positions on rifle butts, I heard the closest thing to an audible voice from God I ever remember hearing. The Lord said to me something to this effect: "Who do you think gave you this assignment, turkey?" "Uh—I guess you did, Lord." "You got it right, bean-head, so get with the program."

I got the message, changed my attitude, started to get excited about what The Old Guard was excited about, and found it to be a rewarding and important assignment with superb soldiers—and by the way, a perfect introduction to the Army for my new bride. It was also a real help in my first post-retirement job as Commandant of Cadets at Culver Military Academy. In this position there was little use for my skills in attacking a hill or campaign planning, but the Culver cadets did a lot of parading, and I knew how to march!"[168]

Persistence

When God intends for us to do something, He is often persistent. We might hear God, but doubt, debate and weigh the pros and cons, sometimes concluding that the instructions weren't right. Faith is not intellectual understanding, but deliberate commitment.[169] We will know that the instructions come from God because of their quiet persistence. Our own ideas often come and go. Cyndi shared that when she was thirteen years old, a fairly new Christian and very serious about her relationship with God, He called her to be a missionary. Here is her story:

"I was walking down the road looking up at the clouds. I was praying and praising God in my mind and thinking about Him. Having been raised in a dedicated Christian home, I had grown up in the church, had a good knowledge of the Bible, and had heard testimonies of ministers and missionaries concerning their 'callings.' All of a sudden, there was a jolt in my mind, heart and spirit and I felt the Lord speak to me, telling me that He wanted me to be a missionary. It wasn't an audible voice, but it was very clear and definite, and as real to me today as it was so many years ago. My first reaction was, 'Oh no! Me? I'm not sure I can do that! What will my friends think of me being such a radical Christian?' But my prayer quickly became, 'Okay, Lord, but you'll have to help me to be obedient when the time comes, because I don't think I'm strong enough to do that!'"

Cyndi went to college and turned away from the Lord in rebellion, interested in worldly pursuits. God was persistent. Eventually, she turned back to Him and realized her life was slipping away. It was time to be obedient to His call from many years earlier. Cyndi became a missionary in Guatemala and has the wonderful feeling now that she is doing exactly what God called her to do.

Sometimes God's plan doesn't match our desire and we resist. Jonah certainly was not interested in preaching to Nineveh, but God was persistent in pursuing him and got him there, via a whale (Jonah 1). Nelfa, Caroline, and Michael shared stories of God's persistent call, even when they were unwilling to heed at first. God got them to the place where they each needed to be.

Nelfa was working for the Philippine government but was unhappy. She wanted to be an artist but couldn't afford to leave her steady source of income. She poured out her heart to God in prayer and heard a quiet voice say, "Work with clay." She hated clay, so kept praying for a different answer. After several months, she agreed to submit to God's voice and embark on a new journey as a potter. It was difficult, and many times she wanted to quit, but mysterious things kept happening to keep her on course. Working with clay eventually became her passion. She has been blessed with many awards, becoming a respected ceramic artist in both the Philippines and in Colorado, where she now lives.

It's important to note that God's calling includes many vocations, not just pastoral or missionary work. God called Nelfa to be a potter. She now praises God that "He made me good" and she desires to serve Him and tell others what He has done for her.

Caroline wrote, "When I was a very new Christian, I began attending Community Bible Study. After a few months, the leaders asked me to be a children's teacher. I thought they were crazy! I knew less about the Bible than the three-year-olds I'd be teaching! So, I said no. I bumped into the leader again a few months later, and she asked me again. Again, I said no. Right before the class was supposed to start in the fall she called me a third time, and said, 'Every time we pray about whom to ask, your name comes up.' I said, 'That's really flattering, but I just don't think that is what I should be doing right now.' I hung up the phone, and God completely froze me. I literally could not move. I sat there stunned for twenty-five minutes. Finally, I realized God was speaking to me, and that I should listen! I was able to move enough to write down the leader's phone number. Once I did that, I could move again! I returned the call, agreed to teach and began a few weeks later. I taught for three years, and then became the children's director for the next eleven years. This is what I needed to be doing. God knew, but I didn't."

Michael had attended church for many years but had never participated in any church activities. One Sunday, his pastor gave a sermon on how there's a place for everyone in the church. A list was provided, and when he looked it over, he didn't see anything that interested him. "I kept going back to the list, and the 'evangelism' category stuck out. My inner thoughts were, 'No, not me, I can't do it. I'm shy and can't speak well in public. For that matter, I can't even speak to one person.'"

Michael went to a meeting about evangelism, and for some unknown reason, signed up for a program called "Evangelism Explosion." He struggled at first, but quickly mastered the training. This was so out of his comfort zone, that only God could have done this. He believes it was God who gave him the confidence and boldness to be successful in this program. He went on to become an Evangelism Explosion trainer. Michael said, "I didn't hear a voice, but it was like there was a force in my mind that kept pushing me in that direction."

You Can Do It

It is common for us to feel unqualified for what God asks us to do. Take a look at some of our Bible heroes: Jacob was a cheater, Peter had a temper, David had an affair, Noah got drunk, Jonah ran from God, Paul was a murderer, Gideon was insecure, Miriam was a gossip, Martha was a worrier, Thomas was a doubter, Sara was impatient, Elijah was moody, Abraham was old and Lazarus was dead.[170] Moses didn't think he was up for the tasks God called him to do. He was timid and unskilled at speaking.

*But Moses said to God, "Who am I that I should go to Pharaoh and
bring the Israelites out of Egypt?" And God said, "I will be with you."*
(Exodus 3:11–12)

*Moses answered, "What if they do not believe me or listen to me and
say, 'The Lord did not appear to you?'" (Exodus 4:1) Moses said to
the LORD, "Pardon your servant, Lord. I have never been eloquent,
neither in the past nor since you have spoken to your servant. I am
slow of speech and tongue." ... "Please send someone else."*
(Exodus 4:10, 13)

Doesn't this sound like our own excuses? "Oh Lord, please send someone
else!" Gideon struggled with God's call too. He was a simple farmer—certainly
not a courageous fighter. Yet God called him to lead Israel into battle. He, too,
resisted.

*"Pardon me, my lord," Gideon replied, "but if the Lord is with us,
why has all this happened to us? Where are all his wonders that our
ancestors told us about when they said, 'Did not the Lord bring us
up out of Egypt?' But now the Lord has abandoned us and given us
into the hand of Midian." ... "but how can I save Israel? My clan is
the weakest in Manasseh, and I am the least in my family."*
(Judges 6:13, 15)

Mary was only a teenager, not a mature, spiritual woman with experience in
being a mother. Yet she didn't argue with the angel who told her that she would
be the mother of Jesus. She was willing to do what God asked.

*"I am the Lord's servant," Mary answered.
"May your word to me be fulfilled."*
(Luke 1:38)

David was also just a teenager, a shepherd. But he saw no problem with slaying a Philistine giant.

The Lord who delivered me from the paw of the lion and the
paw of the bear will deliver me from the hand of this Philistine.
(1 Samuel 17:37)

God can and does use unlikely people to accomplish His purposes. God doesn't call the qualified, He qualifies the called.[171] No matter where you are in your life with God, He is qualifying you for His service because you are called. He can help you overcome the mistakes you have made, and even use them to help others. Paul refers to us as earthen vessels—jars of clay—nothing special when we operate under our own steam. In Jesus, however, we are cracked pots filled with the precious treasure of His Spirit (2 Corinthians 4:7) and His light shines through our cracks. We must have the courage to let the light and love of Jesus shine through us, fanning into flames the gifts God has given us (2 Timothy 1:6–7). When we are dependent on Him instead of our own resources, and put our trust in Him, He will use us to do great things.

Peggy shared this story about her son Josh, a young man who is developmentally disabled, with a diagnosis of fragile X syndrome. He is on the autism spectrum, yet, even in his weakness, God used him in a mighty way.

Josh's parents have been in ministry with teens for over twenty-five years and are often the first called when a family experiences a tragedy. On a cold day in late January, Peggy's husband, Joe, received a call from a local police officer, asking if he would come immediately. A family's twenty-four-year-old son had committed suicide. There were four sons in this family, and one of them had already died at a young age. Joe hopped in the car and left quickly, asking Josh and Peggy to pray for him and the family.

Peggy prayed for wisdom and compassion for Joe so he could walk with this family in their loss. Then Josh started to pray asking God to be with his dad. He suddenly just stopped. Peggy shared how Josh seemed to be in direct communication with God, saying, "yes, okay, I see." He then began talking to God out loud, thanking Him for caring for this man. "Yes, Jesus," he began, "thank you for coming to the woods and scooping him up off the ground and carrying him to God's lap." Josh then turned to his mom and said, "He's okay now, because he's in God's lap."

Joe listened to the family as the father shared how their son had been struggling with depression and had taken his life. The police had found him on the ground, in the woods. Peggy's heart jumped when she later heard Joe's account. Josh had seen it all in his talks with the Lord. No question about it. Neither Peggy nor Josh knew anything about what had happened to this young man, yet Jesus told Josh the kind words that ministered to this family miraculously in their time of grief. "Jesus found him in the woods, scooped him up and carried him to God's lap." Peggy said, "We have always thought Josh had a connection with the Lord, and that his communication was unlike any we had seen. Josh tunes in to the Lord in ways I can only hope to do."[172]

God uses the young, old, sinful, disliked, simple, unattractive, disabled, weary and unskilled, calling them and giving them what is needed to carry out His will. Caleb was eighty-five years old when he tackled giants (Anakites), saying that he was strong and vigorous because the Lord was helping him (Joshua 14). So, don't make the excuse that you are not good enough, not able or not ready. All God needs is a willing heart and He will do the rest. "For God is working in you, giving you the desire and the power to do what pleases Him" (Philippians 2:13 NLT). Will we argue with God like Moses and Gideon, or like Mary and David, will we be courageous and willingly accept His plan? You can do it!

God is our best cheerleader. When we are down and out, He encourages us with just what we need. As a writer, I have learned that over and over. I often feel inadequate for the task at hand, thinking, "Who am I to have knowledge or wisdom to pass on to anyone else?" Yet, God assures me that He is working in and through me to accomplish His purposes. He constantly tells me that He is with me and that I can trust Him.

Nancy didn't feel that she was able to measure up to the task at hand. Both her elderly parents-in-law had become ill and needed her to travel out of state to care for them. She had her own health issues and wasn't very strong. She was sitting on the airplane feeling hopelessly overwhelmed, when she clearly heard Jesus's voice say, "I have equipped you." God spoke to her gently, encouraging her that she could do it and that He would be with her. His words reassured her. However, doubts set in again before the plane landed. Again, she heard, "I have equipped you." Nancy said to herself, "Okay. I've got it."

Nancy got off the plane not knowing what to expect but feeling strongly that God would take care of everything. She knew Jesus would be there to help her care for her elderly parents-in-law who were prone to falling. She knew if they did fall, she couldn't lift them, but God would provide.

The week that she spent with her parents-in-law was remarkable. She was miraculously able to do the necessary care, cooking and cleaning with renewed energy. God protected them from falling. In addition, she was actually able to have fun with them—singing and dancing. The love between both of them and Nancy flowed and filled them all with joy. God's encouragement enabled her to tackle the task at hand, even doing more than what was required.

When we do hear God's call, we need to submit. If we don't have the desire, He will develop it. If we don't have the means, He will provide. If we don't feel adequate, His strength shines in our weakness. If we need reassurance, He will confirm the plan through the affirmation of others. We can be sure that God will guide us and be with us.

"Whether you turn to the right or to the left, your ears will hear a voice behind you, saying, "This is the way; walk in it."
(Isaiah 30:21)

——•⟩ *Stop and Refresh* ⟨•——

1. Are people less spiritual because they haven't heard God actually speak to them? When God wants us to do something, does He always speak in words? What other ways does God use to let us know His will? What is meant by "orchestrating circumstances"?

2. If we are on the wrong path, will God let us know what He wants us to do instead? If so, what are some ways He will do this?

3. What are some ways God uses to let us know His will? Do we always understand it immediately? Read Ecclesiastes 9:10 and Philippians 4:11–13. When we have a restless spirit, is God always telling us it is time to move on? What else can restlessness mean?

4. What does the phrase "God doesn't call the qualified but qualifies the called" mean to you? Do you think this is true? Discuss some of the people in the Bible who were not up to the task. How did God provide for them? How does this relate to you?

5. What if God asks us to do something we don't want to do? What is His part? What is our part?

Chapter Twelve

LOST

Learning to discover God's will

"For I know the plans I have for you," declares the LORD, "plans to prosper you and not to harm you, plans to give you hope and a future."
(Jeremiah 29:11)

What if we take a wrong turn on our journey? What if we are unclear about what God wants? What if we are struggling to know His will, and He is not revealing it to us? We may cast about struggling to find God's plan for our lives becoming frustrated and anxious. What if I miss His perfect will for me? I'll be doomed to a life of unfulfillment and unhappiness. It would be nice if God just wrote His will on a marquee with neon lights. Then there would be no question.

God is faithful. He will direct us and teach us, but we need to pay attention to where He is leading. "This is what the LORD says—your Redeemer, the Holy One of Israel: 'I am the LORD your God, who teaches you what is best for you, who directs you in the way you should go. If only you had paid attention to my commands, your peace would have been like a river, your well-being like the waves of the sea'" (Isaiah 48:17–18).

To seek God's will, we must first seek Him. We fail when we place our own ideas, our own service projects, and even our own holiness and character before our desire to know God.[173] But it is still difficult to hear Him sometimes and know where He is leading. The six A's—Ask, Anticipate, Ask Again, Acknowledge, Accept, and Act—can be helpful tools in helping us discover God's will.

Ask

"Ask and it will be given to you; seek and you will find; knock and the door will be opened to you" (Matthew 7:7). When we trust God, acknowledge Him and go to Him in prayer, He has promised to direct our paths (Proverbs 3:5–6) and give us the needed wisdom (James 1:5). But, asking God for something has requirements. We must remain in His presence. We must want to hear Him all the time, even when things are going well and life is uneventful. If we ignore God's directives or make it a practice to handle life on our own most of the time, He will stop speaking to us and guiding us. If we only seek God when we are in trouble, or when the decision is so important that we finally need His help, we may find that He is silent. However, if we come before Him with humbleness and repentance, we will find He is a gracious, forgiving God who does not treat us as we deserve to be treated.

Anticipate

We should expect and believe that God will speak to us and guide us. Anticipate His answers and look for Him, not just by a still small voice, or in the Bible, but in all sorts of ways and places. He can use books, magazines, TV and radio, friends and family, teachers, prophecy, nature, circumstances and even more unlikely means like an audible voice, dreams, visions and angels to communicate with us. In the Bible, He even spoke through a donkey (Numbers 22:28)! Chapter thirteen explores ways God has spoken to people today. Let's not limit Him but be open to whatever means He might wish to use to speak to us. Don't let your skepticism or practicality blind you to ways God is working.

Peggy shared that God spoke to her through her husband. He told her God was telling him that she should go back to work. She didn't want to, because she had two small boys, and liked being a stay-at-home mom. He continued to persuade her to consider this, emphasizing that he felt this was from God. Finally, needing to resolve this difference, she put a fleece before the Lord. Her biggest concern was the care of her boys. So she told God that if it was His will for her to go back to work, He would have to provide a babysitter.

At church the next Sunday, she made a conscious effort to avoid people, afraid that someone would make an offer. That following week, she received a call from a friend, who had a son close to her boys' ages. She said she didn't know if Peggy was thinking of going back to work or not, but if so, she would be willing to care for the boys. Peggy hung up the phone and cried. God had provided for her need, unsolicited. It appeared that it *was* God's will for her to go back to work.

After a few years on the job, Peggy advanced to a place where she was making a good salary and receiving benefits. Suddenly, her husband's job ended. Peggy's income got them through that tough financial time. They never missed a house payment and could pay all their bills. God knew their needs. God knew what was coming. He prepared them and provided for them.

Ask Again

If we still are unclear about God's direction, or think we haven't heard from Him, we should get back on our knees. We should ask Him to examine our hearts and lives to see if anything in us is blocking His voice. Ask Him to help us be patient if we need to wait. (Psalm 139: 23–24; Psalm 40:1) Ask Him for His peace. Gideon wished to be clear about God's direction in his life, so he put out "fleeces" (Judges 6:37–39). Like Peggy, we can use this practice to clarify God's instructions too.

Sherryl and Dick used fleeces to confirm an unlikely move in their lives. Sherryl tells their story: "Approaching retirement, my husband and I had been contemplating an out of state move but weren't sure this was something that was in God's agenda, or even something we really wanted to do, for that matter. I wanted to move to a different department within the company where I was working and continue my career for a while longer. It was down to two of us for the position and I felt certain the job would be mine.

Meanwhile, we visited our son's church and during worship there was a man who spoke in tongues. A few minutes later there was an interpretation. I have only heard tongues a couple of times, but when the interpretation was spoken, it was God talking directly to me. No one else, just me! I was told in no uncertain terms that God would be opening a door and He would be closing a door, *this year*. The very next day I learned that I was not selected for the position at work. That was the door closing. If God wants to move fast, He can certainly do so. Now we knew that I should retire.

We were still unclear about moving. Over the next several months, God kept telling us to move forward. We had a list of twenty-two 'God-things' that had to happen before we would move—our fleeces. I didn't hear God Himself speaking. He used other people, actions and events, but He was speaking to me all the same, beyond a shadow of doubt. It became very clear that we should move—the open door. It was amazing how God orchestrated each part of this move, and how He provided for every need."

Acknowledge

When we hear from God, we must acknowledge with faith that it is He. It's easy to brush Him aside, thinking we are misinformed. Our reason strives to prevail. Once we believe that God is indeed saying something, it's important to notice all the ways God may be confirming His message to us and acknowledge those too. Be receptive to His speaking and leading, however it may come. Don't limit

Him. Often God will give us the same message in two or three different ways from two or three different sources. I have been amazed at God's emphasis on a topic when I'm writing devotions, asking Him for His words to speak through me to people. I read five other devotion books and a passage from Scripture. Many times the same concept is reiterated over and over again, and I know that is what He is wanting me to write.

Seek the counsel of godly friends too. (Proverbs 15:22). They can be invaluable in helping us sort things out. We must remain in prayer, asking for God's peace, and acknowledging that we're ready to do His bidding.

Accept

God may ask us to do something we don't want to do. His ideas may be different from ours and may even be different from what logic says and others think. We may find ourselves in isolation as others shake their heads at our folly. God's way is not majority rules. Remember, God's wisdom may appear as foolishness (1 Corinthians 2:14). Sensibility is not always a characteristic of God call. Do we say, "Yes I will obey God if what He asks of me doesn't go against my common sense, but don't ask me to take a step in the dark?"[174] Our soul has gotten out of intimate contact with God when we lean on our own religious understanding. We should get in the habit of continually seeking His counsel on everything instead of making our own common-sense decisions and asking Him to bless them. Don't walk in your own light but walk in His light. If a person is ever going to do anything worthwhile, there will be times when he must risk everything by his leap in the dark. Trust completely in God, and when He brings you to a new opportunity or adventure, offering it to you, see that you take it."[175] When God calls, accept what He is asking you to do.

David determined on New Year's Eve that his word for the year would be "Yes." No matter what the circumstance, he would say yes to God without argument or hesitation. It wasn't long before his decision was challenged. He was asked to go to Jordan to write about the plight of Christian Syrian refugees. He had been to Jordan once before and vaguely knew one person and had the phone number in his pocket for emergencies. He contacted the American consulate with his plan. With two weeks' vacation from his postal service job, he bought a plane ticket and was on his way, on his own.

He stayed in a hotel—American by name—but rather seedy. He couldn't sleep, so he sat in the lobby in the middle of the night drinking coffee. "How would he ever contact refugees?" he wondered. He knew no one. But God had it covered. A young boy approached his table and said "Hi". "You speak English?" David asked, amazed. "What is your name?" The young boy was Jack. David knew by his name that he was Christian, not Muslim. As they talked, David learned that his family were Christian Syrian refugees, staying in the hotel because someone had given them some money for a place to stay for a few days. Here was the needed connection.

Jack went and got his father and they spent the rest of the night talking. God was faithful in providing. Over the next two weeks David was able to visit many Christian refugees, thanks to the family he met in the hotel. He learned that they were outcasts in most countries and had no place to go. They were abused and persecuted. Their living conditions were deplorable. Through David's articles, and later his TV and radio appearances, he was able to have a part in alerting the world to their horrible situation.

This is just one of many incredible stories that occurred during David's "yes" year. He's now writing a book called *Just Say Yes: Ordinary People, Extraordinary Living*. Amazing things will happen when we are willing to step out in faith, believing.

Act

Once God communicates with us and lets us know what He expects, we must do what He says. We are told to be doers of the Word, not just hearers (James 1:22). We don't hear God and then weigh the directives to decide whether or not this fits what we want to do. We must obey, all the time, when things are going well and when we are challenged. Many times the window of opportunity is short, so we should act and not delay (Psalm 119:60). God is gracious, however. If we mess up, He'll give us do-overs.

Todd told me about an experience he had before leaving Colorado for the mission field in Honduras. He was working as a maintenance man and involved in an apartment ministry called Apartment Life. God gave him a do-over.

"One day I was making a regular stop at Home Depot and I saw a man getting into his car. I clearly heard a voice, a still, small voice, though not audible, simply say, 'Heart condition.' That was it. I knew I needed to pray for this gentleman. I froze and allowed my fear to stop me. As he drove away, I confessed to the Lord that I hadn't obeyed Him. I didn't experience any guilt or condemnation from Him, but I asked Him for a do-over.

A few weeks later, on Easter Sunday, my wife and I were running into the grocery store. Outside the store sat a lady in her motorized power chair. As soon as I saw her, I heard the Lord speak to me—the same voice I'd heard at Home Depot. He said, 'I am *so* proud of her and I love her so much.' He also said, 'This is your do-over.' I knew this was God.

My wife and I went straight over to her, and I told this lady what the Lord had told me to tell her. She sat there with her mouth wide open for a few seconds and then burst into tears. She cried for a few minutes and we put our hands on her and prayed for her.

When she composed herself, she told us that she had been alone at her home on Easter morning watching church on TV, too embarrassed to go out because of her motorized cart and her weight. As she sat there she asked the Lord if He was still there and if he could send an angel or something to show His presence! What? The Lord used me to give her the answer she needed? He was there, and He told her that He was *so* proud of her! We were all blown away!

Now I always know that voice and for the most part respond to it every time. As soon as we recognize that that still small voice is from Him, we will realize He has been talking to us for a while and that He talks to us often!"

God's will isn't always making a specific choice. Sometimes the choice itself is inconsequential. The most important part of finding God's will is being in relationship with Him, acknowledging Him and responding in obedience. God's will isn't some ethereal calling that one either finds or doesn't. It's living in His presence on a day-to- day, moment-by-moment adventure, listening to His voice and following what He directs. God may lay many choices before us and allow us, in our free will, to choose: what college, what mate, what career, what vacation, what place to live, etc. It may be God's will that we have a great part in determining our path through life. This does not mean that He is not with us.[176]

Linda was in a quandary. She was faced with a difficult, controversial decision and was unsure of the right way to go. She turned everything over to God, telling Him that she was a sinner and that she desperately needed His help and guidance. She prayed for about three hours. When God's answer came, it was not what she had expected. God said, "I will be with you no matter what you decide to do."

God develops our character by allowing us to decide. A child cannot develop into a responsible, competent human being if he or she is always told what to do."[177] God may also give us choices to test us to see *how* we will choose. Do we choose what is best for us or what is best for God's kingdom?

"God sometimes allows you to get into a place of testing where your own welfare would be the appropriate thing for you to consider, if you were not living the life of faith… The greatest enemy of a life of faith in God is not sin, but good choices which are not quite good enough. The good is always the enemy of the best… Many of us do not continue to grow spiritually because we prefer to choose on the basis of our own rights."[178]

God can bless us in many choices if we remain connected to Him and keep Him in the equation. God is concerned about both the significant and insignificant events. If we are not listening, we will miss opportunities, not see open doors, not recognize circumstances and, most of all, not experience God. Jesus tells us to remain in Him so we can "bear much fruit" for apart from Him we can do nothing of value (John 5:15).

"At first, we want the awareness of being guided by God. But then as we grow spiritually, we live so fully aware of God that we do not even need to ask what His will is, because the thought of choosing another way will never occur to us."[179]

God's will is defined as living in His presence, not being sucked into the world's standards, but letting God develop us into the person He intended us to be. The apostle Paul wrote, "Do not conform yourselves to the standards of this world, but let God transform you inwardly by a complete change of your mind. Then you will be able to know the will of God—what is good and is pleasing to Him and is perfect" (Romans 12:2 GNT). As we develop this kind of relationship with God, we will hear Him clearly without question. Charles Stanley wrote that people who have truly heard from God need no convincing. They have perfect peace. They simply know that the decision was of God."[180] When we are in tune with God, we don't have to struggle, wondering what to do or where to go. God keeps us in perfect peace, when our minds are stayed on Him (Isaiah 26:3 NKJV).

Following God's will is an adventure. All sorts of endeavors, accomplishments, experiences and ministries open up so unexpectantly that we can only say they were of God, not ourselves. We have exciting things to see.

We continually ask God to fill you with the knowledge of his will
through all the wisdom and understanding that the Spirit gives, so
that you may live a life worthy of the Lord and please him in every
way: bearing fruit in every good work, growing in the knowledge
of God, being strengthened with all power according to his glorious
might so that you may have great endurance and patience.
(Colossians 1:9–11)

──•◦ *Stop and Refresh* ◦•──

1. Read Proverbs 3:5–6, Proverbs 16:3, Proverbs 19:21, and Romans 12:2. What are some requirements for understanding God's will? Will God always bless our plans if our intent is to serve Him? Why or why not?

2. Read Judges 6:37–39. What does it mean to "put out a fleece?" Do you think this is a valid method for determining God's will today? Why or why not?

3. Is God's will always a particular decision? How can we define God's will? In addition to what you have learned in this chapter, read 1 Thessalonians 5:18, James 4:13–15, and 1 Peter 4:19. What do these verses say about God's will? Why does God allow us to make our own decisions? Is that good? Why or why not?

4. If we think God is asking us to do something that is risky and is opposed to what others think, should we stop? Is logic a characteristic of God's will? What would happen if you decided to say yes to God? Is that reasonable?

5. If you followed what you thought was God's will, and it didn't turn out well, were you wrong? Why or why not? How can we know? In times like these, what does God do for us?

Chapter Thirteen

SIGHTSEEING

God has so much to show you.

Come and see what God has done, his awesome deeds for mankind!
(Psalm 66:5)

Wake up sleeper. Shake off the cobwebs and release all the muck that entangles you and holds you back. The landscape stretches before you with so much to see. Look, hear, and learn. God is your guide. He is anxious to show you what He is doing and what He has planned. He's excited to watch you learn and grow. Com'on. Let's go!

Many of us have trouble laying aside our practicality, skepticism and reason. We want proof. We scrutinize and dissect. If something is out of the ordinary, we want to examine it to see if there is a reasonable explanation. We even want to attribute miracles to some natural or human cause, or even coincidence or good fortune.

When I was discussing the people of Israel crossing the Jordan River after God stopped the water, a friend commented that there must have been a significant logjam upstream because of the flood. Others have told me that this is merely a symbolic story, not an actual event. This way of thinking blinds us to God's involvement in our world. We fail to acknowledge His presence and His work. 1 Corinthians 3:18–19 reminds us that God's wisdom often appears as foolishness to us. We cannot understand God and His actions solely with our intellect. We need faith. Like Balaam (Number 22:31), we are so involved in our own agendas that we don't see what God is doing, and don't give Him the credit when something happens. Balaam was so frustrated by his donkey's lack of cooperation that he didn't see the reason. Once his spiritual eyes were opened, he saw an angel standing there. Let's ask God to open our spiritual eyes of faith so that we can notice how He is working in our lives.

Other folks, as Pastor John described in the Forward, feel like they are on the outside looking in. Though they want to hear God, they've not heard Him with the same clarity that others describe, and they feel unworthy or left out. It is important to remember that God loves each of us equally with an unfailing love and will communicate with each of us in His unique way. Don't try to replicate another's' experiences, or pursue the experience itself, but seek God Himself and discover the special way He wants to communicate with you personally. He is there for you.

We have already seen many ways that God can communicate with us. He uses His Word, the Bible and the Holy Spirit's still small voice. Other people and various media sources can also deliver His messages. God works through circumstances to direct us. But, there are numerous other ways He interacts with us. We will see examples of His presence in nature, songs, angels, visions, dreams and word pictures. This is by no means an exhaustive list. God is incredibly creative and tells us what He wants to say in all sorts of ways, so don't limit Him. Be watching and listening.

Nature

"Keep close to nature's heart… and break clear away once in a while, and climb a mountain or spend a week in the woods. Wash your spirit clean."[181]

In our travels, we love to view God's wonderful creation: the high mountain peaks and beautiful waterfalls; the towering cliffs and colorful rock formations; the vastness and power of the sea, and the wide and fruitful expanse of the plains. Everywhere we look, God's creativity, power, and care are evident. I often want to break out in a chorus of "How Great Thou Art."

Our house has a view of the mountains, and we can watch storms coming and clouds rolling in. When I read Psalm 121:1–2: "I lift up my eyes to the mountains—where does my help come from? My help comes from the Lord, the Maker of heaven and earth," I envisioned God in the clouds, pouring over the mountains in power, coming to my aid. I wonder if something similar inspired David to write those words.

David wrote frequently about God's character evidenced in nature. Take a look at Psalms such as 65 and 104 where he vividly describes God's hand in nature. God uses the world around us to teach us truth about Himself and deliver messages to us. People have shared stories with me about God speaking to them through nature.

My friend had been having a rough week. It seemed like everything was against her. She took some time to relax by hiking in the woods, and when she rounded a bend, two bald eagles were sitting on a log. Wishing she had her camera, she took a deep breath at the rarity and beauty of these majestic birds. She stopped and watched for a few minutes until they flew away. As they went, she heard God speak. "Don't worry, I am with you. You and I can soar together." Since then, she says that she sees pairs of birds everywhere, reminding her that she and God are in this together.

Val has suffered through a past of repeated trauma. Her self-esteem was damaged, and she has dealt with a lack of love. God has made it a point to send her "Val-entines." She sees heart-shaped items everywhere she looks: rocks, clouds, potato chips, cookies, dryer lint, dental floss and even dog pee in a litter box! Hardly a day goes by without her heart reminder. She says a silent prayer every time: "Thanks, God. I see it. I love you too."

Roy wrote that several years ago, on a Sunday in February, he had a frustrating day. Things weren't going smoothly. He and his wife decided to drive to church in separate cars so he could take care of some things first, but they took longer than planned. He was late. As he drove, it seemed he hit every stoplight and was behind every slow Sunday driver.

By the time he pulled into the church parking lot—quite late—he was frustrated and angry. He wasn't sure that he could go inside the church and worship when he was so out of sorts. As he sat there in his car, a mourning dove landed in the parking spot next to him. Mourning doves aren't usually around in February. The dove walked around a little, then cocked its head so that one eye looked directly at him. Then he heard these words, "Be at peace, Roy." The words were as clear as if someone was sitting in the car beside him.

The dove flew away and Roy decided to go into church, still not sure that he was in the right mood for worship. As the service progressed, he could feel the anger, the frustration and finally all of his anxieties fade away. He left the service in peace. Since that day, Roy has come to realize that God is with us all the time, and He cares about the things that concern us.

God can even use nature to resolve a problem. Johnna wrote that when she was nineteen, she was working at a summer camp, and some disturbing things happened. She went for a run and was looking up at the clouds, thinking about the issues and God. The sky looked very strange with just one odd-looking cloud in the middle of it. As her attention was drawn to the cloud, she felt a peace, which she believes was from God. He let her know that she shouldn't worry because He would resolve the problem.

My neighbor says that sunrises and sunsets are the best way she experiences the presence of God. The Bible tells us that the heavens declare the glory of God and the skies proclaim the work of His hands (Psalm 19:1). The vast expanse of stars shows us a mind-boggling view of God's immensity. Romans 1:20 tells us that we can understand God's attributes through nature. Look around and appreciate what you see and listen for God speaking to you through His creation.

Songs

You are my hiding place; you will protect me from
trouble and surround me with songs of deliverance.
(Psalm 32:7)

Several years ago, I took the K-LOVE radio challenge: listening to only Christian music for thirty days. As a talk-radio junkie, this was a difficult change, yet I decided to see if listening to Christian music alone would really change me. I had been uptight, impatient and had difficulty sleeping. After just a few days, I did begin to notice a difference. I was sleeping better. I was calmer, less angry and less critical. Maybe there was something to this.

As I listened, I often heard testimonies of radio callers who told how God had spoken to them through a song, allowing them to hear what they needed at just the right time. I have found this to be true over and over again in my life also. But God doesn't just speak through Christian songs. Remember, our God can do anything and use any means to get through to us.

Fred likes to listen to the oldies. He was playing music from the Moody Blues and the song "Nights in White Satin" came on. The chorus played, "And I love you, yes I love you, Oh how I love you, oh how I love you." God spoke and said, "Fred, that's the way I feel about you."

Angels

For he will command his angels concerning
you to guard you in all your ways.
(Psalm 91:11)

All though the Bible, people encountered angels. Sometimes there was just one, sometimes two or three, and maybe a whole host. They appeared in dreams, in physical form as ordinary people, or as beings of light or flames of fire. They came to deliver messages from God, to warn, to encourage, and to tell the future. They came to protect and minister to those in need. God used them to carry out His judgements. Usually they showed up briefly and disappeared, but sometimes, as in the story of Abraham, they lingered. (Genesis 18–19) Most of the time, they weren't expected, and their recipients were amazed, even fearful. In a few cases, such as in the story of Balaam, they were invisible, and not seen until God "opened the spiritual eyes" of those involved. (Numbers 22:31, 2 Kings 6:17) They weren't always recognized. Sometimes they were delayed because of battles with evil spiritual forces (Daniel 10: 12–13). If you are interested in researching all the occurrences of angels throughout the Bible, use a search engine such as Bible Gateway and look for "angel" or "messenger." They occur more frequently than you might think. Here are a few descriptions of angels from Scripture:

- They are stronger and more powerful [than we are] (2 Peter 2:11).
- Angels are "ministering spirits sent to serve those who will inherit salvation." (Hebrews 1:14).

- "Do not forget to show hospitality to strangers, for by so doing some people have shown hospitality to angels without knowing it" (Hebrews 13:2).
- "Then I looked and heard the voice of many angels, numbering thousands upon thousands, and ten thousand times ten thousand" (Revelation 5:11).

Several people have shared stories about angels appearing in our times. Some survey responders mentioned angels appearing in dreams. In most cases, they appeared as ordinary people, and their angelic status did not become evident until after the fact. Who would've thought that an angel would drive an old woody station wagon, wear jeans or appear in a too-small state trooper uniform! It seems their most common function is providing help when we are in trouble and in need of power beyond ourselves. In a few cases, they provided encouragement and peace. Though skeptics could explain away the evidence of angels as a natural occurrence, the fact remains that, angel or not, God provided help at precisely the right time in an amazing way. Here are a few of the many stories. You decide.

As a child, Annette remembers being outside playing hide and seek with friends. While running to "home base," she turned and ran into the handlebar of a baby carriage and knocked herself flat. She lived on the top floor of the apartment building nearby and remembers a large man carrying her up seven flights of stairs to her mother. He promptly disappeared before her mother could thank him. "How did he know where I lived and where did he come from?" Annette later asked herself. "I believe he was sent by God to help me."

There was another time as an adult that Annette believes she saw an angel again. She was driving their Suburban with her injured husband and seven children in the car. She was eight months pregnant. The car had a blowout going seventy mph on I-75. Not panicking, she took her foot off the gas and coasted over to the side of the road. She cried out to God for help, knowing she could never change the tire herself. When she opened her eyes, a state trooper was there, dressed in a beige uniform—not the typical dark green uniform of a Florida state trooper. He was wearing a large brim hat over his bald head, and was huge, towering over her, his biceps busting out of his rolled up uniform sleeves. It seemed like God had sent a big angel and had to stuff him into an earthly trooper uniform. The man bent over the Suburban rear tire and with his bare hands, not electric tools, jacked up the car, turning the tire iron and removing all the bolts so fast the she was shocked. It only took about fifteen minutes to change the tire. She looked up to thank him and he was gone—no sound of him leaving, no car engine revving, nothing. She looked up and down the highway and he was nowhere to be seen. No one else in the car remembered seeing him. Annette believes he was an angel, sent to help her.

Marion, a retired pastor's wife, told me a story about seeing an angel while she was in rehab after surgery for a broken leg. Here is the story she wrote:

"After some surgery I spent a few days in rehab at the Covenant Village Health Care facility. The first night I woke up and needed a bathroom trip. I rang for help which was slow in coming. Finally, I cried out complaining, "Lord, help me. I am so helpless. I can't do a thing for myself." The words of Isaiah 41:10 assured me that the Lord would help me. As I laid on my bed looking at the dark ceiling, an angel face appeared. It was a little face with snug curls all around the sweet chubby face. Surprised, I wondered what was going on. I closed my eyes and when I opened them, the angel was still there. This happened three times. I began to feel a sense of peace.

Shortly after, a big handsome black man came into the room. I said, 'Oh, thank you for coming to help me. My name is Marion, what's yours?' He answered, 'Moses.' He assisted me into the wheel chair and to the bathroom and back again into bed. I thanked him for helping me and he left.

When the day shift nurse came on duty, I told her, 'I really appreciated that black man who helped me during the night. I'd like to thank him.' After some thought she said, 'Marion, there was no black man on duty last night! We have no one on staff named Moses.' I believe Moses was an angel sent to help me."

Here is another story from Marion: "Our family celebrates reunions every three years and this year my grandkids were in charge. As I prepared for it, I was fearful. After all, I was almost ninety years old and I wondered what room I'd have, how close I would be to the bathroom, and how would I get along using a walker on the uneven mountain terrain. I wanted everything to go well without incident.

When we checked in, the people at the registration desk assured me that I was close to the bathroom. Other problems such as traversing the rugged mountain terrain were taken care of with help. I was satisfied with my room situation. As I crawled into the lower bunk bed and was comfortably set for the night, on the ceiling, through the upper bunk, I saw an angel with a long flowing gown and flowing hair. I was surprised, but the angel gave me the assurance that God was with me, and that He was taking care of me. God took away all my fears. Why should I be afraid when I have His promise that He will never leave me or forsake me? Praise the name of Immanuel, God with us!"

Kent shared a story about his encounter with angels. They appeared as ordinary men and came on the scene to offer needed assistance.

"It was a rainy, wet afternoon. My wife Donna and I left a restaurant where we had just enjoyed having lunch with friends. They went on their way, and we braved the elements to make our way slowly to our car. My wife has limited sight and suffers from severe rheumatoid arthritis that compromises her balance. As I guided her down an incline to where the car was parked, she slipped on the wet pavement and fell. I leaned down to help her, and suddenly two older men appeared. One helped me lift her. I turned around to thank them, but they were gone. I couldn't believe they had left so quickly. I looked around the parking lot and toward the door of the restaurant. The cars in the lot were unoccupied, and none were moving towards the exit. After I got my wife situated in the car, and thinking that the men might have gone into the restaurant, I went back in to thank them. The hostess said no one had entered since we left. I had no idea where they had gone so quickly.

As I thought about this later, I believe these men were angels that God sent to help us in our time of need. My wife described being lifted as floating up like a feather, a rather extraordinary sensation.

Wes was in a serious predicament. He needed help and God provided. Here is his story. He was traveling from one town to another. The shortest route by far was through a mountain pass. It was early December, and though the pass was officially closed for the season, the weather was sunny, so he figured it would be safe to use the pass. Understandably, there were no other cars on the road.

As he neared the summit, his truck hit an ice patch and he careened off the pavement, rolling over and over, down a steep ravine. Amazingly, he was able to get out of his car and climb the steep embankment back up to the road. As soon as he reached the pavement, an old woody station wagon pulled up, driven by an older man wearing a flannel shirt and jeans. The man asked if he needed help. Wes asked him for a ride to the nearest town so he could hire a tow truck.

The elderly gentleman didn't say very much, but dutifully drove him to a service station that had a tow truck sitting on the lot. Wes got out of the car and headed into the shop, suddenly realizing that he had not thanked the man. When he quickly turned around, the car was nowhere to be seen—not visible down the road either way, or anywhere in the lot. Wes asked the attendant if he had seen the car, hoping he might recognize it since it was so unusual. The attendant hadn't seen anyone drop him off.

Wes is now convinced that this was an angel. He disappeared too quickly without a trace and had arrived on the scene precisely when Wes needed help. Wes is grateful to God for protecting him in this accident, and providing the help he needed, even though he'd acted foolishly.

God provides help in all sorts of circumstances. Lynn told about a time when she and her husband went on an elk hunting trip. The weather turned frigid. They shot a very large cow elk and did the usual preparations for transport back to the car, which was two miles away. Lynn's husband, Roy, volunteered to hike back to the truck to get the travois, to assist them with carrying the elk, while Lynn stayed behind to start skinning off the hide. Suddenly she slipped, and her fall caused her to go into shock. She tried to stay alert and warm—bouncing, wrapping herself in the silver emergency blanket, and even laying on the elk body for warmth, but she felt she was not improving. Suddenly two men walked up and told her she looked as pale as a ghost. They quickly went to get Roy. The men found him and hurried him along. That was the first saving grace from God. It was unbelievable that these men showed up in such a remote area, just when Lynn needed help. Roy brought back the needed supplies.

It took them two days to butcher the heavy elk into moveable pieces that they could carry back to the truck, in freezing snow, and up and over a steep hill. The hide alone weighed seventy pounds. At one point the temperature reached fifteen degrees below zero. With half the task done they almost gave up but noticed a small car with a man sitting in it. He introduced himself as "Adam" and greeted them like a friend. They told him about their predicament and how difficult the task had become. He said he was waiting for a friend but would be happy to help them carry the elk to their car. Roy and Lynn reiterated the difficulty, but he insisted that he could do it. They looked at each other suspiciously but after some discussion accepted his help. This stranger was tall, strong, energetic and kind. He helped them get all the meat back to the truck in a couple of hours, with seemingly little effort.

Hardly believing how capable he was, they of course offered him meat to take home and some cash. He only accepted one small package of elk. They thanked him emphatically for doing a job that they thought was impossible. While packing the back of the truck, they turned to once again thank him and tell him that they hoped he would find his friend, but he and his car were silently gone! After reflecting on how secluded they were, the difficulty of the situation, their fatigue, and the cold penetrating their bodies, they could only surmise this had been an angel sent by God to help them. Lynn said, "That man disappeared but left behind a memory of thankfulness we could only attribute to God's awareness of our predicament. We just never know when and where and how God will let us know He is fully aware of our lives."

Missionaries such as Dr. Virginia Blakeslee have told stories about being surrounded by an army of angels, protecting them from the assaults of cannibals.[182] They were unaware of their supernatural protection until they were told about what the natives saw. We are often out of tune with the spiritual forces that surround us too. We can be assured that God is watching over us and sends his guardian angels to protect us and help us, even when we don't see or acknowledge them. I am trying to be more in tune to the influence of guardian angels, thanking God each time I avoid a close call.

Visions and Dreams

> *I will pour out my Spirit on all people. Your sons*
> *and daughters will prophesy, your old men will*
> *dream dreams, your young men will see visions.*
> (Joel 2:28)

It was normal for God to speak in dreams during Bible times. Jacob, Joseph, and Daniel are probably the most noted dreamers of the Old Testament, whereas Peter and John in the New Testament are also known for their dreams and visions. All through the Bible, we see people who had unusual dreams with alternative meanings that needed interpretation, as well as dreams where God spoke clearly. Kings such as Nebuchadnezzar employed wise men for the very purpose of dream interpretation.

Our culture typically doesn't place a lot of credence in dreams, and few people in the United States see visions. These are much more common in third-world countries where the opportunities to encounter God through church and the Bible aren't as prevalent. I was surprised at the number of responses to my survey that indicated people have heard from God in dreams. Though God has not appeared to me in a dream, I have found that when I walk more closely with God the themes of my dreams change.

Several people who responded to the survey mentioned seeing a light, a corner of a robe or a hand while praying. This wasn't disturbing, but comforting, letting them know God was with them. April had a dream about Abraham and Sara when she was going through a particularly stressful time in her life. In the dream, God said, "Have faith." The message came through loud and clear and was just what April needed. This provided her with the comfort and peace she needed to get through the difficulty.

One of the survey takers told of a dream in which he was visited by God and Jesus—he did not see the Holy Spirit. He had been praying for the gift of tongues prior to an evangelistic crusade at his college. The idea of the event intimidated him. In the dream, God and Jesus were in the air searching for him. When they found him, they descended, and he began speaking in tongues. He was startled and woke up. He found that he was really speaking in tongues. That night, his fears vanished, and he was able to participate with the energizing power of the Holy Spirit at the evangelistic event.

Ed shared two different reoccurring dreams which he believes shaped his decisions. The first series happened while he was in college. He was dating a girl and had gone to her college town for the weekend, where she was babysitting. The child's parents weren't home, but she had a girlfriend with her. In the middle of the night, the friend laid down next to Ed, but wanted an invitation to get under the covers because she was cold. He was most distraught and considered getting his tent and sleeping bag from the car and "camping" in the back yard, even though it was winter and there was snow. After a lengthy "stalemate" she finally quietly left.

Throughout the rest of the weekend, Ed subtly expressed his disapproval of the friend, while still being civil. The weekend activities were not to Ed's liking—alcohol and a bar scene. Though they did go to church, Ed had reservations about the relationship with his girlfriend. They broke up a few months later.

Ed had been having a reoccurring dream for a few months prior to this in which he was a helper at a church, preparing things for Sunday. He placed hymn numbers on the board. When he looked at the church bulletin to identify the hymns, he noticed someone was getting married. On closer examination, it was He. He went into panic mode, not wanting to marry an unknown girl. The dreams continued throughout this dating relationship, and each time, as the marriage seemed more imminent, his panic increased. The dreams ended when they broke up. Ed believes this was God letting him know that he should not consider marriage to this girl.

Oddly enough he had the dream again after he met the girl who is now his wife. This time, he was walking to the church with his father, but felt very confident in the knowledge that he was to be married there. There was no panic. Ed believes this final dream was God's announcement of His wonderful gift to him in the person of Gail, who is now his wife.

Ed told me about another dream he had following their ninety-five day round the world honeymoon, visiting weather stations and Lutheran missions. He had been busily serving in his church back home, but his personal relationship to God had faded. A new series of dreams started in which he was driving a car up a hill and it started sliding backward. Pressing the brakes didn't help. With each episode, the backward motion was increasingly more difficult to stop, and eventually he was even approaching the edge of a cliff. His panic increased as the car kept moving backward.

He understood these dreams to mean that he was backsliding in his faith and needed to fix this. God was warning him. He experienced gradual healing through the messages on a Christian radio station. This got him back on track, strengthening his faith and helping him serve God more passionately.

God used a dream in Johnna's life to help her forgive a boyfriend who was cheating on her with her good friend. She had been angry and resentful. In the dream, the couple were in the front seat of a car and she was in the back seat. They all were having a pleasant conversation. When she woke from the dream, she was at peace and had forgiven them completely.

Dennis had a warning dream about his church. It happened twice and involved some problems with the church leadership. The second time, the dream was actually a vivid vision while he was at work. These dreams sparked a church restructure which eventually caused them to dismiss their pastor and deal with some serious underlying problems. Danyce had a similar dream about her church, and this helped her be prepared and at peace when things started to get "wonky."

Several people shared that their dreams seemed to tell the future. It appears that dreams about impending catastrophes such as automobile accidents or heart attacks are common. God used these dreams to prepare people to handle situations with resolve, strength and peace.

God may give us windows into our future through our dreams or other means. I was told about dreams where people saw their children to be or witnessed a situation that hadn't yet happened. It didn't have an impact until later when it came true, and the dream was remembered. It is important to not seek God for the future, however. Although He sometimes will let us know what is going to happen, God considers our pursuit of the future to be evil, especially when we use means other than Him to discover our fate. Take a look at the displeasure He showed in the Bible when people sought the advice of spiritists, witches, and mediums (Deuteronomy 18:10–12; Leviticus 19:31 and 20:6; Galatians 5:19–21). God wants us to trust Him for our future and walk by faith, not by sight. (James 4:13–15).

Word Pictures

Jesus spoke all these things to the crowd in parables; he did not
say anything to them without using a parable. So was fulfilled
what was spoken through the prophet: "I will open my mouth in
parables, I will utter things hidden since the creation of the world.
(Matthew 13:34–35)

When Jesus was on earth, he frequently talked in parables—word pictures that painted a story to illustrate a point. Many of these parables were confusing and left people wondering about the meaning. Sometimes Jesus explained the principle to his disciples.

Several people have indicated that God speaks today in word pictures too—giving us an image that illustrates what He wants to say to us. The difference seems to be that we immediately "get it." These pictures usually speak to our current situation.

I was thrilled when Connor DeFehr, Pastor of Worship and Family Ministry at FSB Church of Northglenn, CO, sent me several pages of his journal. It is evident God speaks to him regularly through a still small voice, Scripture, dreams and word pictures. It was an honor to share his experiences. I have picked out a few of my favorites from his long list of word pictures.

Connor saw a yellow bouncing ball with purple stripes. It was malleable without being changed itself. God used this to tell him to take the punches, but allow himself to bounce back immediately, confident of his original shape.

He saw a picture of people as wheels that needed to be renewed, changed, and filled with air. The breath of the Spirit provided the needed air that sustained the people. Without the air, God's people were less effective and slower at their tasks because they had not surrendered to the wisdom and guidance that comes from the Spirit.

Our desires (flesh) are like a mosquito bite that needs scratching. We instinctively follow after selfish, fleshly desires, but just like scratching a mosquito bite, the more we attend to them, the worse they become. Avoiding them is really in our best interest.

God's promises are like a climbing wall. We can pull on the rocks as we climb, they bear our weight, and we won't fall.

People at church are like carrots stuck in the ground. It is easier for them to remain safe and secure. But, they must be taken out of the ground and eaten by the world so that God may become known to others through His gift of the Spirit.

Connor said that each of these pictures addressed something that was going on in his life at that moment. Though not as frequently, God has also used word pictures when I am praying to underscore His truth.

In one, I saw hundreds and hundreds of gifts. God told me not to open just my hands, but to receive His bounty with my arms wide open, taking all that I could carry.

In another, God showed me a picture of a puppy, bouncing after his master with enthusiasm, tail wagging. God said that that was how He wanted me to follow Him.

Perhaps my most involved word picture was more of a story. I was climbing a very tall mountain, traversing boulder fields and snow fields, carefully going over crevasses and steeling myself against the forces on wind-swept ridges. He told me He was my Sherpa. He knows the way through the wilderness. He wanted me to move forward, carefully placing one foot in front of the other, following His lead. He would find cold mountain streams where I could drink deeply and be refreshed, and He would allow me to take rest breaks when I became weary. On slippery places, He offered me His hand. "You will reach the summit and the view will be glorious," He said, encouraging me.

Danyce wrote about a time when God wanted her to pray for a person in a group. All the ladies appeared as flowers, facing to heaven. One flower, however was wilted and being trampled by a boot. Although she appeared fine on the outside, Danyce later learned that this lady was in a bad place in her life.

When we are in prayer, when we are around people, when we are facing problems, we can ask God to reveal to us what He wants to say to us personally, or to us about others. Be ready for whatever means He wishes to use.

I hope you are as amazed and inspired by all these stories as I am. God wants to speak to us and will use many means, so don't limit Him or shut Him out. Perhaps these stories will give you ideas of how you might better hear Him, so you are more aware. God is lovingly and caringly desiring an intimate relationship with His people. We only need to pay attention.

Now then, stand still and see this great thing
the Lord is about to do before your eyes!
(1 Samuel 12:16)

1. What are the primary ways that you have heard from God? Have you had any unusual occurrences? Would you be willing to share? Have you heard others' stories that you could share?

2. Do you hear God on a regular basis? As you pay attention to Him, how has that affected your communication with Him?

3. Why do you think Jesus used parables so often in His ministry? How does God use the things around us today to teach us truths about Himself?

4. As you have read this book and gone through this study, what is the most significant thing you have learned? Has your relationship to God been enhanced so that you can hear Him better? How? Read chapter fourteen. What is God doing in your life? How can you pass this on to others?

5. Where will your journey take you from here? Have you made a commitment to believe in Jesus? If so, speak with a pastor or Christian friend that can help you as you move forward. Have you made a commitment to walk more closely with Him? What steps do you plan to take following this study so your relationship with God will continue to grow?

Chapter Fourteen

MAKING MEMORIES

Remembering and pondering the awesome deeds of the Lord

I remember the days of long ago; I meditate on all your works and consider
what your hands have done.
(Psalm 143:5*)*

My journey to a closer walk with Jesus in which I could hear His voice more clearly, began in 2009 when my husband and I began attending a new church. I tried to seek God regarding what ministry I should pursue, but nothing seemed to ignite my passion. Needing to talk to God, I took a walk along a lake path with my dog, praying as I went. She was an Aussie Shepherd mix who stayed right beside me but became annoyed if I stopped or deviated from the pace and route. As we hiked along, I asked God for direction. The word "write" kept coming to my mind. "But, Lord, write what?" I asked. I had no known outlet or ministry that fit this category. I stopped for a moment to argue with God, and my dog nudged me along impatiently. I needed to move forward, but how?

Later, back at church, I became involved in a variety of service projects, but I felt restless. Nothing fit. I kept praying, and "write" kept coming to mind. Two years later, Perry and I met with our pastor, John Martz, to discuss my grandson's upcoming baptism. He suddenly stopped midsentence. He told me that the woman who posted our church prayer line on email had fallen and broken her leg. She could no longer do this ministry. Would I be interested? I asked what it entailed. Pastor John told me I would need to compile all the prayer requests that were turned in to the church and *write* a short devotional. It was as if a lightbulb turned on in my head. This was what God was calling me to do.

At first the ideas for the devotions came easily, but after a few months, I was hitting a wall. I decided to start praying for ideas, also asking God to use me to touch the lives of people who read that post. I became amazed at the ways God spoke to me, showing me truths about Himself and His Word in ordinary, everyday situations. I called these "God-sightings." It seemed that everywhere I went, God was there, teaching me through unlikely places and activities: gardening, cooking, driving, mopping the floor and doing laundry, to name just a few. God was faithful in providing ideas each morning, when I didn't know what to write. When I prayed, thoughts that were far from my normal consciousness, just popped into my mind. It was even more incredible that almost every Sunday, people commented that God had touched their lives by one of the devotions I had written that week—my prayers were answered!

Eight years later, spurred on by the encouragement of my readers, Cladach Publishers help me publish a book of devotions: *Everywhere I Look, God is There.* I have been blessed by the feedback I've received. God continues to use these devotions to speak into people's lives with encouragement, hope and motivation. I'm humbled that God is using me as a conduit to convey what He wants to say to people.

Writing devotions began my journey to a closer, more intimate, conversational relationship with God. As I continue to do this, I am excited to see what He will do every day. I'm keeping a journal, recording my concerns and God's responses. God continues to astonish me as this relationship develops.

At first it was a little weird and strange, but as I learned to hear God's voice, the conversation became easier and easier, and I was blessed by this relationship.

I learned so much about God, the Bible came alive, and my quiet time with Him was no longer a chore. I eagerly looked forward to time with Him, much like I anticipate a lunch date with a close friend.

This is the relationship I want to share with you. God won't necessarily act the same way with you as He has with me, but I'm convinced that He desires a communicative relationship with each of His children. When you seek Him, you will find Him and discover that He will do remarkable things in your life. You will begin building a legacy that you can pass on to inspire others.

I'm so grateful to the people who had the courage and impetus to share their stories with me about God speaking. Many have expressed that they want to help others through what they have experienced, so they are delighted to pass these on. They have inspired me tremendously. As I thank them, I also give thanks to God with awe that He is dealing with people in such a caring and intimate way.

When God showed me a word picture of hundreds of gifts and told me to open my arms wide to receive them. I had no idea that He would shower me with such an abundance—more than six hundred responses on the survey, a wonderful crew of dedicated writers who have volunteered to help proof, correct and critique my work, and others who have encouraged me and prayed for me. I would've been lost without them.

A friend's son likes to do databases. He set up my survey and helped analyze the data. I had no idea that he was talented in this regard. Friends and family provided an extensive network, passing along this survey to their friends and family. I don't even know six hundred people, so here was another miracle. God has provided.

I was in the grocery store recently and ran into a former neighbor. Her son, whom I remember as a little squirt, is now a college sophomore, studying computer science. His hobby is web design. I had no idea. He filled a need I had of designing a web page. He set up my website and a blog and answered numerous techie questions. I am so computer-challenged, but God provided for this need when I wasn't even looking. There are no coincidences with God.

Over and over again, God shows up with guidance, wisdom, help and inspiration. I have learned to look for Him and respond with praise. He is working all around us if only we would pay attention and take the time to notice.

It is my prayer that you have been inspired to embark on a journey to a closer, more intimate relationship with God. He loves you and is waiting for you. I would love to hear from you via email or on my website: stepintheriver.com. Share your concerns, but also share the wonderful things God is doing in your life. Do step in the river. A wonderful promised land awaits where you too will praise God for His mighty acts on your behalf.

> *Give praise to the LORD, proclaim his name; make known among the nations what he has done. Sing to him, sing praise to him; tell of all his wonderful acts. Glory in his holy name; let the hearts of those who seek the LORD rejoice. Look to the LORD and his strength; seek his face always. Remember the wonders he has done.*
> (1 Chronicles 16: 8–12)

Appendix

SURVEY RESULTS

605 Responses

T he survey responses are mostly from people who consider themselves Christian. Many have not indicated a denomination. The young people (12–17) were mostly from church youth groups. The least amount was the 18—25 age group, and the most was over fifty-five probably because that group includes the majority of our friends. Twenty-five states and six foreign countries have been represented. It has been suggested that males who answered the survey may not be a good cross-section, for only certain males would be interested in responding to a survey.

Survey Participants' Ages

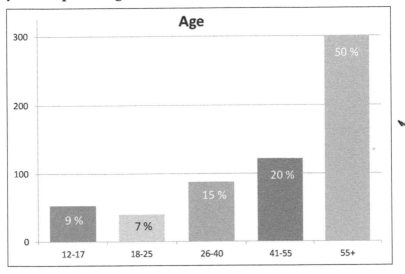

Survey Participants' Genders

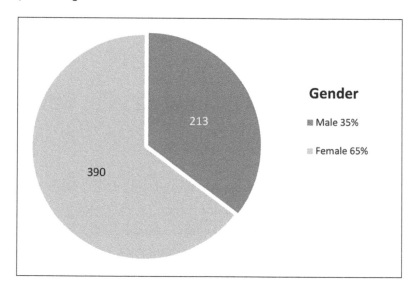

Religious Affiliations

39 different religious affiliations were listed, however most respondents were not specific and listed themselves as "Christian," "Non-denominational," or "Unaffiliated."

Self Reported Religious Affiliations

Anglican	Church of Christ	Interdenominational	Pentecostal
Assembly of God	Church of God	Latter-Day Saints	Protestant
Baptist	Episcopal	Lutheran	RLDS
Believer	Evangelical	Messianic	Salvation in Christ alone
Bible-based church	Evangelical Covenant	Methodist	Somewhat Christian
Born-again Christian	Evangelical Free	Mystic	Spiritual
Buddhist	Friends	Nondenominational	Taoist
Catholic	Full Gospel	None	Unaffiliated
Christ-follower	Independent	Not sure	Unitarian Universalist
Christian	Love Jesus	Presbyterian	United Church of Christ

Occupations

If retired people indicated their former occupation, that was included instead of "retired."

   Business (78): executives, owners, managers, administrators, marketing, sales, public relations, communications, human resources, non-profits, consultants, analysts, coaches, administrative assistants, corporate relocaters, real estate, property managers

Finance (20): accounting, actuary, bookkeepers, research funding, bankers, tellers, cashiers, insurance brokers, retail, waiters

Technology (11): IT, web design, graphics, systems engineers

Law Enforcement (9): attorneys, paralegals, judicial deputies, law enforcement officers, probation officers

Publications (20): Writers/authors, editors, printers, publishers, photographers

Construction (6): engineers, architects, machinists, electricians, landscapers

Scientist (5): chemists, earth scientists, scientists, lab managers

Health Sciences (38): nursing, EMT, doctors, optometrists, dentists, phlebotomists, nutritionists, dietary aides, x-ray techs, physical therapists, health and safety, health care, health sciences

Social Sciences (20): counselors, therapists, speech therapists, counseling assistants, social workers, mental health care, psychologists, psychiatrists

Care-givers (60): child care, elder care, home aide, housekeeping, homemakers

Education (168): teachers, professors, coaches, trainers, tutors, administrators, secretaries, librarians, para educators, bus drivers, international student hosts, students (k-12, college, advanced degree, seminary)

Ministry (41): pastors/ministers, spiritual directors, youth/children's ministry, ministry support staff, missionaries, community outreach

Military and pilots (15)

Retired

Miscellaneous: automotive mechanics, automotive fleet, manicurists, volunteers, disabled, postal workers, parks and recreation, tourism, none

How do you define your spirituality?

It is evident that most of the survey responses were from those who either regularly attend church or are deeply committed to their faith. Some responses included comments that they had quit going to church because of shame, ridicule, and condemnation, but tried to remain in their faith without church. The categories in this question were:

Not spiritual

Mildly spiritual, but not religious (do not attend a place of worship)

Occasionally attend a place of worship

Occasionally attend a place of worship and practice some additional spiritual activities

Regularly attend a place of worship, but no additional spiritual activities

Regularly attend a place of worship and practice some additional spiritual activities

Deeply spiritual and practice several additional spiritual disciplines

The first chart groups only those who responded to one of the first four categories. This was less than ten per cent of the total. The next two charts show all categories by age and gender.

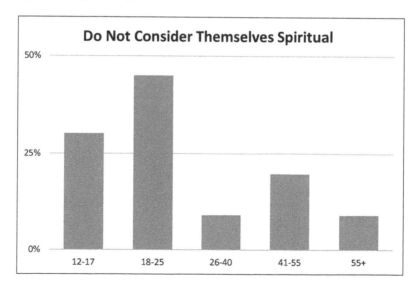

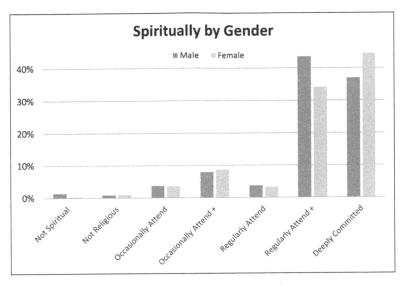

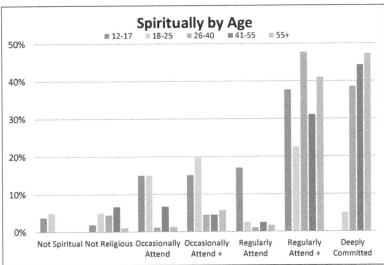

Other responses to this question were:
- Have strong beliefs but do not attend church (4)
- Do not attend a place of worship but talk to God on a regular basis (1)
- Personal relationship with Jesus: (3)
- Spiritual and a Christ-follower but do not practice religion (2)
- Spiritual and healing practices daily center my life (1)
- Church is when two or three are gathered together (1)

Do you believe God speaks today?

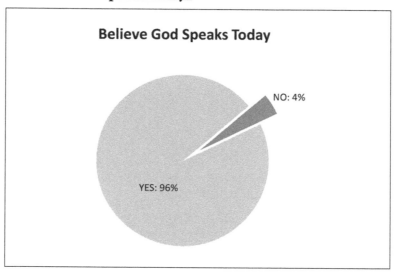

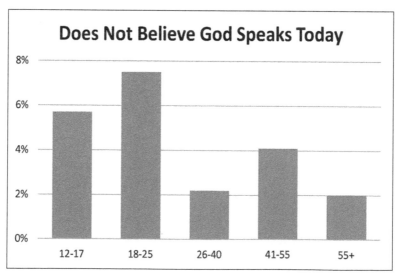

Why doesn't God speak today?

- Doesn't exist
- Not sure if there is a God
- Not sure He speaks
- Has already said everything He is going to say in His word
- God has set the world in motion and is watching from afar

- God doesn't speak because of sin
- Doesn't have a personality, just a force
- We don't need God, we have been given the authority to decide
- God has His hands full so doesn't usually speak to us
- Speaking is a human construct
- Our own spirituality speaks within us through deep emotion
- We can be spiritual without God

How does God speak today?

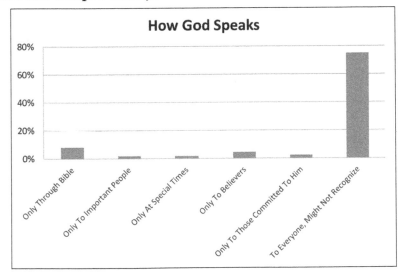

Write-in responses:
- Speaks to everyone in all sorts of ways
- We can't limit God, not bound by our ways
- God is infinite so we can barely understand Him
- He speaks through modern prophets
- He speaks through nature
- He speaks through the Holy Spirit
- He speaks whenever He wants to
- He speaks to seekers

Do you want God to speak to you?

Yes: 98.3 percent; **No:** 1.7 percent

Why don't you want God to speak to You? (11 responses)

- It frightens me
- Not sure it is God
- Will condemn and criticize
- Prefer to be on my own
- God is only a force
- People need to change
- People erroneously talk about God speaking
- I don't know

Ways God speaks to us today

This data is arranged by those who believe God could speak in a certain way and those who have *actually experienced* this method. Age groups and genders are compared. Some interesting findings:

There is not a great deal of difference between genders and age groups, except that the 12–17 age group is significantly lower in most categories (except dreams and signs). The 18–25 age group also tended to be lower but scored higher than all other groups in hearing God by signs. The highest overall scores were in the 26–40 and 41–55 age groups. This can probably be attributed to the fact that the people responding to the surveys in those age groupings indicted deeper overall spirituality. Males and females were very close in their responses, however males experienced God more by nature and females more by songs. The two highest categories were by scripture (average 90.7%) and answered prayer (average 91.7%). The number of people believing God speaks in dreams and visions, as well as experiencing them, surprised me.

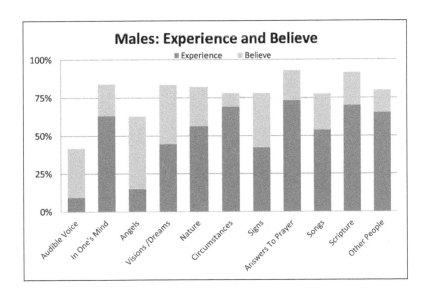

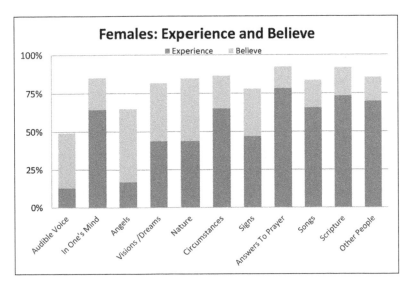

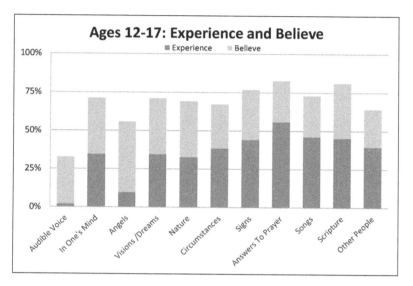

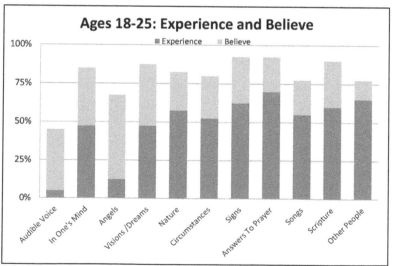

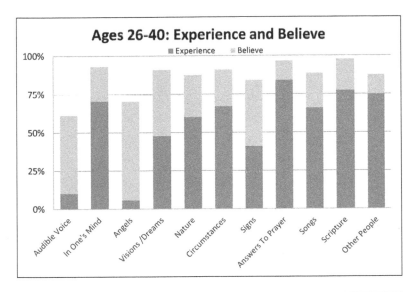

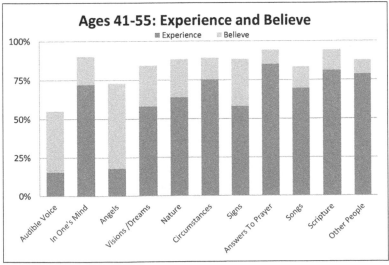

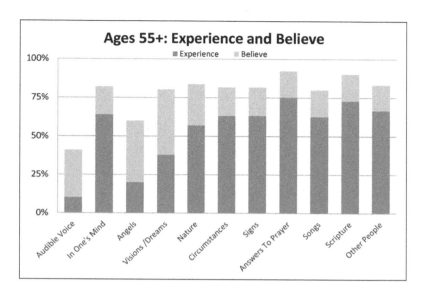

What do you want God to talk to you about? (592 responses)

People in all genders and age groups were most interested in both praying about and having God talk to them about guidance, encouragement, comfort, peace, and truth. Males scored lower than females in all categories except truth. The least interest was in life after death, God's character, and conviction or confession. I was surprised at the higher percentage of 12-17s who were interested in life after death.

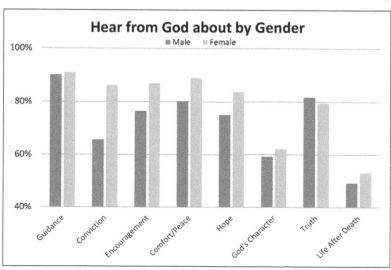

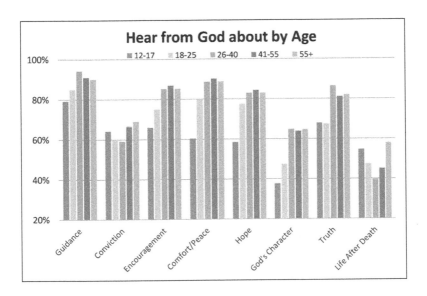

<u>When and how often do you pray?</u> (591 responses)

Most people pray daily or continually. If people *only* listed grace or bedtime, those are noted, although those single categories are not well populated because many included grace and bedtime in a list of other things. The final two categories are those who only pray for requests or help.

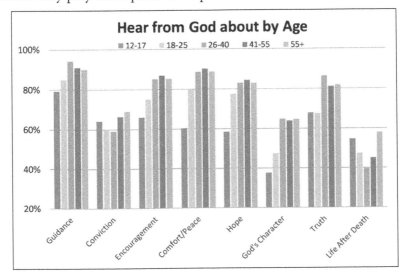

What do you pray about? (591 responses)

There is insignificant difference between age groups and gender. As before, the 12–17 age group and the 18-25 age group had lower percentages. Only 92 percent of the 12–17s responded , whereas 97–99 percent of the other groups responded. I was surprised that across the board, people were more likely to pray for others than for themselves.

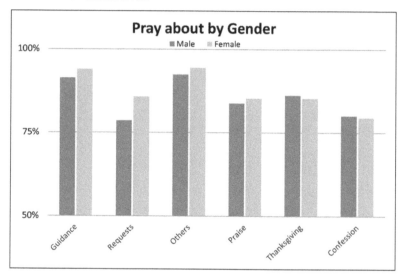

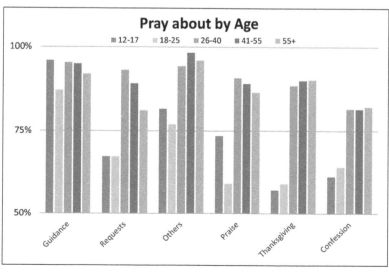

<u>Are you frustrated with prayer?</u> (115—25.7%)

- Am I doing it right, does it really work? (3)
- Not sure of the connection, awkward, difficult because we can't see Him (5)
- I'm not consistent (2)
- Get distracted (9)
- Too impatient, slow, delayed (17)
- Confused because bad things happen (3)
- Nothing changed (3)
- Don't understand the answers, confusion, not clear (11)
- God doesn't hear me, my prayers aren't answered, don't get what I want (45)
- God helps those who help themselves (3)
- Don't know how to pray, need to learn (4)
- People write prayers, not God (1)
- God wants a relationship, but it is too hard (3)
- Want to hear God's audible voice (1)
- Answers are different than what I expect (3)
- Not logical or predictable (1)
- Is prayer relevant? (1)

<u>Why do you pray?</u> (Optional question, 420 responses)

- For comfort, peace, feel better, soul nourishment
- To connect with God, to talk, communicate, have a relationship, to hear God
- To become aware of His presence
- Helps me pay attention to God, know Him better
- To get help when I need it
- To make requests, God uses prayer to answer us and help us.
- It changes me, refocuses, aligns me to God, become more like Jesus
- It lifts my burdens, makes life better
- Without prayer, there is a void in my life.
- A privilege that allows me to speak directly to God

- Commanded to pray, Jesus set example, necessary discipline, habit
- Reveals things, gives guidance, wisdom, insight, clarity, understanding
- Because I love God
- Helps me reach beyond myself to something bigger
- Express gratitude, praise
- It's fun
- Exhausted all other options
- Don't know, doesn't seem to work

How do you make special time for God? (Optional question, 477 responses)

Many responses indicated that they did not make time, have time, or couldn't because of attention problems. Some said they were too selfish and possessive of their time. Others said that no special time was needed because God will speak when He wants to speak.

- Alone, quiet, be still, solitude, kids are asleep, intentional time out
- Get away, "War Room," retreat
- Attention to God's presence, purposeful listening, asking questions and waiting, looking for signs
- Tarot cards
- Journaling
- Reading God's Word, reading devotions
- Sermons, spiritual leaders, mass
- Praying, fasting, speaking in tongues
- Meditation, reflection, mantra, imagination
- Nature, outside, woods
- Driving, walking, jogging, running, working in the yard, biking
- Hot tub, bath, shower
- Falling asleep, sleeping
- Music, worship, praise, adoration
- Sharing with friends
- Anytime it is needed
- Learning how

How do you discern it is really God? (Optional question, 443 responses)
Several people indicated that they can't tell, don't know how and can't be sure.
They observed that we will not be right 100 percent of the time. Many wished
they could better discern.

- Sense God's presence
- Aligns with the Bible truths (God's Word), God's promises
- Aligns with God's character
- Sense of peace
- Just know, a gut feeling, intuition
- His ideas are bigger, better, wiser, smarter than ours
- His ideas come from a different part of your mind—way back
- Confirms our ideas
- Circumstances, open doors, results, signs that happen out of the blue
- Message is confirmed in other ways, and by other people
- Persistence, pushes, leads, urges, compels, won't let us be
- By faith, belief
- Physical sensations: tingling, heat, smells, jolts, paralysis
- Learn to discern by practice and experience so that you just know
- Different quality of voice that we learn to recognize
- Risky, something we don't want to do, something we didn't think about, uncomfortable, unexpected, off-the-wall
- Ask and wait for an answer, it is apropos

ACKNOWLEDGMENTS

How can I begin to acknowledge anything without first pointing to my awesome God. He has been faithful beyond measure. I am also hugely indebted to my dear husband, Perry, who has tirelessly proofed, commented, critiqued, encouraged, and prayed for me.

In addition, there are some others I would like to mention specifically.

I wish to thank my editor, Deb Hall, who worked patiently with me through this process, sharing her expertise. Matthew Nelson designed and processed my survey. Vicky Reier also helped with the survey questions. Kyle Coffey designed my website. Each of these people, experts in their fields, did outstanding work.

Colorado Writers on the Rock and the Colorado Christian Writers Conference have provided helpful information to jump-start this process. Our Arvada group of WOTR has been a wonderful source of encouragement and information.

I have appreciated my proofers who read and commented on my chapters, giving me direction and helping me sort through some of the more difficult concepts. In addition, several people have helped wherever needed. There have been many in this category—friends, family, my bible study group, and church members. A few have truly gone above and beyond in this respect, so I would like to mention them by name: Michelle Arbuckle, Val U Able, Jim and Pat Burdick, Carol Cassell, Ed and Gail Holroyd, Regina Macy, Kent and Donna Nelson, Jeff and Jana Osterlund, and Lynne Stephens. Special thanks to Pastor (Dr.) John Martz who started me on this journey and wrote the foreword for this book.

I cannot say thank you enough to all the people who took the time to take the survey. I am especially indebted to those who have had the courage to share their stories about God speaking. This book couldn't have happened without their submissions.

Finally, this process wouldn't have been successful without prayer support. People were praying, and this was my needed inspiration in times of discouragement, writer's block, and feeling overwhelmed. God honors and answers the prayers of His people. Thanks to you all.

ABOUT THE AUTHOR

 Susan Roberts grew up in Massachusetts, one of four children. She thanks God for the strong Christian influence in her childhood home. She attended Wheaton College in Illinois, where she received a bachelor's degree in English and secondary education, and later a master's degree in interdisciplinary studies including Christian education, family studies, and communication. Sue met her husband, Perry, at Wheaton, and they were married on Front Campus, heading out after graduation to a life in the military.

As a military wife, Sue was active in the post chapel programs as a board member of PWOC (Protestant Women of the Chapel). She had numerous speaking engagements with the chapel, PWOC, and Christian Women's Club. She was a Bible study leader and taught both adult and children's classes. She was a children's leader with Bible Study Fellowship.

As a mom of three children—Carol, Chris, and Kurt—she was also active in PTA, school activities, and their soccer teams as a referee, coach, and team mom. All the kids are now married to wonderful spouses. She has five exceptional grandchildren.

Sue loved to explore interesting places at each military duty station and planned frequent outings to discover history, nature, and other interesting places. Her local friends who accompanied her were amazed to see things they didn't know existed, even after growing up in that area. Her other hobbies have included crafts, gardening, and cooking.

When Perry retired from the military, they moved to Colorado. Sue recently retired after twenty years with the Jefferson County School district as a school secretary. Sue has continued her love of travel, researching, and planning trips. She and Perry have now visited all fifty states and would like to visit all the National Parks, getting stamps and ranger autographs in their passbook. In the summer of 2017, they visited their Air Force son, Chris, and his family in Ramstein, Germany, spending six weeks touring sixteen countries.

Sue is continually amazed at the beauty and diversity of God's creation. Seeing and hearing God everywhere has been a passion of hers, and she has collected stories from people who share this passion. Sue writes a weekly devotional based on "God sightings" for the Arvada Covenant Church prayer line. In January 2017, she published, with Cladach Publishers, a compilation of these devotions in a book called *Everywhere I Look, God Is There*. Other devotions and articles have appeared in online publications. Her vision is to help others on their journey to develop a deeper relationship with God through her writing, speaking and teaching.

You may contact Sue through her website, stepintheriver.com, using the contact page to go to her Facebook or her email. You are also invited to check out her blog, accessed through the webpage.

ENDNOTES

Chapter One

1   David G. McAfee, http://www.patheos.com/blogs/
    friendlyatheist/2018/02/16/joy-behar-is-right-if-you-think-god-is-literally-
    talking-to-you-seek-help/#9U6D80ZZ4FDBGp0c.99.

2   *The View*, Season 21, Episode 103, produced by Bill Wolff, featuring
    Whoopi Goldberg, Sunny Hostin, Joy Behar, Sara Haines, Paula Faris,
    Meghan McCain, aired February 13, 2018 on ABC.

3   Eric Metaxas, *Breakpoint Daily*, (Colson Center for Christian Worldview),
    February 27, 2018.

4   T. M. Luhrmann, *If You Hear God Speak Audibly, You Usually Aren't
    Crazy*, CNN Belief Blog, December 29, 2012, http://religion.blogs.cnn.
    com/2012/12/29/my-take-if-you-hear-god-speak-audibly-you-usually-
    arent-crazy/.

5   Ibid.

6   Ibid.

7   Eric Metaxas, *Breakpoint Daily*, February 17, 2018.

8   Joel Anderle, *The Covenant Home Altar* (Chicago: Covenant Publications,
    2017), 2013.

9   Christopher Yoder, September 15, 2015, "On Paying Attention," *Commentary on Liturgy; Augustine, Confessions 10.27.38.*

Chapter Two

10   Francis Thompson, *The Hound of Heaven,* (New York: Morehouse Publishing, 1988).

11   Brian and Sally Oxley, Sonja Peterson and Devin Brown, *The Hound of Heaven, a Modern Adaptation,* (Ft. Forward Meyers, FL: Oxvision Films, 2014).

12   Francis Schaeffer, *The God Who Is There* (Downers Grove, Illinois: InterVarsity Press, 1998).

13   Augustine, *Confessions, Article 15,* translated by Rex Warner, (New York: Mentor, 1963).

Chapter Three

14   Brian Flood, *OprahsayssheswaitingtohearfromGodabout2020run afterJoyBeharmockedPenceforlisteningtoJesus,* aired February16, 2018, (Fox News).

15   Frans du Plessis, secular humanist, *Does Not Believing in God Make Me a Bad Person?* ("Quora").

16   Oswald Chambers, March 7, *My Utmost for His Highest* (Grand Rapids, MI: Discovery House, 2015).

17   Catherine Marshall, *Moments That Matter* (Nashville, TN: Thomas Nelson, 2001), 231.

18   J. I. Packer, *Knowing God* (Downers Grove, IL: InterVarsity Press, 1973), 37.

19   Dallas Willard, *Hearing God* (Downers Grove, IL: InterVarsity Press, 2012), 193.

20   Elizabeth Elliot, *God's Guidance* (Grand Rapids, MI: Baker Book House, 1997), 66.

21   Catherine Marshall, *Moments That Matter* (Nashville, TN: Thomas Nelson, 2001), 28.

22   Oswald Chambers, April 28, *My Utmost for His Highest* (Grand Rapids, MI: Discovery House, 2015).

23   Catherine Marshall, *Moments That Matter* (Nashville, TN: Thomas Nelson, 2001), 253.

Chapter Four

24   Patricia Raybon, November 29, *God's Great Blessings* (Grand Rapids, MI: Tyndale House Publishers, 2011).

25   C. S. Lewis, *Problem of Pain* (San Francisco, CA: HarperOne, 2015).

26   Oswald Chambers, May 20, *My Utmost for His Highest* (Grand Rapids, MI: Discovery House, 2015).

27   C. Austin Miles, *In the Garden, The Gospel Message No. 2* (Philadelphia, Hall-Mack Company, 1912).

28   Dallas Willard, *Hearing God* (Downers Grove, Illinois: InterVarsity Press, 2012), 146.

29   Dietrich Bonhoeffer, *Cost of Discipleship* (New York, New York: Touchstone Books, 1995).

30   A.J. Gossip, 1873-1954; (Arthur John Gossip, Professor of Christian Ethics and Practical Theology at the University of Glasgow from 1939 until 1945).

31   Oswald Chambers, July 7, *My Utmost for His Highest* (Grand Rapids, MI: Discovery House, 2015).

32   Ibid., July 11.

33   Dietrich Bonhoeffer, *Cost of Discipleship* (New York: Touchstone Books, 1995).

34   Ibid.

35   Catherine Marshall, *Moments That Matter* (Nashville, TN: Thomas Nelson, 2001), 208.

36   Bill Hybels, *Too Busy Not to Pray* (Downers Grove, Illinois: InterVarsity Press, 1998), 45.

37   Ibid., 43.

38   Catherine Marshall, *Moments That Matter* (Nashville, TN: Thomas Nelson, 2001), 184.

39 Sarah Young, *Jesus Calling: Enjoying Peace in His Presence* (Nashville, TN: Thomas Nelson, 2004), 26.

40 Priscilla Shirer, *Discerning the Voice of God* (Chicago, IL: Moody Publishers, 2012), 57.

41 Dietrich Bonhoeffer, *Cost of Discipleship* (New York: Touchstone Books, 1995).

Chapter Five

42 Sarah Young, *Jesus Calling: Enjoying Peace in His Presence* (Nashville, TN: Thomas Nelson, 2004), 147.

43 Doug Dameron, *Is God Even Listening?* (Brighton, CO: Orchard Church, Reasonable Doubts series, April 14, 2018).

44 John MacArthur, *Necessities for Effective Prayer*, (sermon on January 23, 2011) https://**www.gty.org**/.../41-58/**the-necessities-for-effective-prayer**.

45 Catherine Marshall, *Moments That Matter* (Nashville, TN: Thomas Nelson, 2001), 333.

Chapter Six

46 Charles Schultz, *Teen-ager Is Not a Disease* (Salem, MA: Pyramid Books, 1972).

47 David McCasland, *Our Daily Bread* (Grand Rapids, MI: Our Daily Bread Ministries, 2017), October 30, 2017.

48 George Müller, *Soul Nourishment First* (The George Müller Foundation, Müller House, 7 Cotham Park, Bristol, UK BS6 6DA, May 9, 1841).

49 Charles Stanley, *How to Listen to God* (Nashville, TN: Thomas Nelson, 1985), 45.

50 David Platt, *Radical* (New York, New York: Multnomah Books, 1984), 28.

51 Conrad Mbewe, pastor of Kabwata Baptist Church, *The God Who Speaks* (Amazon Video, February 1, 2018).

52 Dallas Willard, *Hearing God* (Downers Grove, IL: InterVarsity Press, 2012), 210.

53 Ibid., 212.

54 Kevin DeYoung, pastor of Christ Covenant Church, *The God Who Speaks* (Amazon Video, February 1, 2018).

55 Priscilla Shirer, *Discerning the Voice of God* (Chicago, IL: Moody Publishers, 2012), 32.

56 David Golinkin, "Torah is as Sweet as Honey" *The Jerusalem Post*, May 22, 2007.

57 Charles Stanley, *How to Listen to God* (Nashville, TN: Thomas Nelson, 1985), 92.

58 Priscilla Shirer, *Discerning the Voice of God* (Chicago, IL: Moody Publishers, 2012), 61.

59 Catherine Marshall, *Moments That Matter* (Nashville, TN: Thomas Nelson, 2001), 294.

60 "What is Lectio Divina?", Wikipedia, *https://en.wikipedia.org/wiki/Lectio_Divina*.

61 Dallas Willard, *Hearing God* (Downers Grove, Illinois: InterVarsity Press, 2012), 48-51.

62 Priscilla Shirer, *Discerning the Voice of God* (Chicago, IL: Moody Publishers, 2012), 31.

63 J. I. Packer, *Knowing God* (Downers Grove, IL: InterVarsity Press, 1973), 19.

64 Charles Stanley, *How to Listen to God* (Nashville, TN: Thomas Nelson, 1985), 86.

65 Oswald Chambers, January 3, *My Utmost for His Highest* (Grand Rapids Michigan: Discovery House, 2015).

66 Ligon Duncan, chancellor of the Reformed Theological Seminary, *The God Who Speaks*, (Amazon Video, February 1, 2018).

67 Priscilla Shirer, *Discerning the Voice of God* (Chicago, IL: Moody Publishers, 2012), 26.

Chapter Seven

68 Sarah Young, *Jesus Calling: Enjoying Peace in His Presence* (Nashville, TN: Thomas Nelson, 2004), 198.

69 Bill Hybels, *Too Busy Not to Pray* (Downers Grove, IL: InterVarsity Press, 1998), 11.

70 Tim Johnson, *The Covenant Home Altar* (Chicago, IL: Covenant Publications, November 10, 2017).

71 C. S. Lewis, *Letters to Malcom, Chiefly on Prayer* (San Francisco, CA: HarperOne, 2017).

72 Oswald Chambers, February 28, *My Utmost for His Highest* (Grand Rapids Michigan: Discovery House, 2015).

73 Sarah Young, *Jesus Calling: Enjoying Peace in His Presence* (Nashville, Tennessee: Thomas Nelson, 2004), 83.

74 Ibid., 205.

75 Oswald Chambers, June 14, *My Utmost for His Highest* (Grand Rapids, MI: Discovery House, 2015).

76 Mark Batterson, *Chase the Lion* (Sisters, OR: Multnomah Publishers,Inc., 2016)

77 Ibid., March 30.

78 Sarah Young, *Jesus Calling: Enjoying Peace in His Presence* (Nashville, TN: Thomas Nelson, 2004), 62.

79 John MacArthur, *Necessities for Effective Prayer* (sermon on February 23, 2011), https://**www.gty.org**/.../41-58/**the-necessities-for-effective-prayer.**

80 Ibid.

81 Ibid.

82 Doug Dameron, *Is God Even Listening?* (Brighton, CO, Orchard Church: Reasonable Doubts, April 14, 2018).

83 J. I. Packer, *Knowing God* (Downers Grove, IL: InterVarsity Press, 1973), 79.

84 Bill Hybels, *Too Busy Not to Pray* (Downers Grove, Illinois: InterVarsity Press, 1998), 39.

85 Ray Vander Laan, *Faith Lessons on the Promised Land,* (Focus on the Family Films, *That the World May Know,* 1998).

86 Catherine Marshall, *Moments That Matter* (Nashville, Tennessee: Thomas Nelson, 2001), 127.

87   Doug Dameron, *Is God Even Listening?* (Brighton, CO, Orchard Church: Reasonable Doubts, April 14, 2018).

88   Sarah Young, *Jesus Calling: Enjoying Peace in His Presence* (Nashville, Tennessee: Thomas Nelson, 2004), 183.

89   Bill Hybels, *Too Busy Not to Pray* (Downers Grove, Illinois: InterVarsity Press, 1998), 15.

90   Ibid.

91   Ibid., 38

92   Oswald Chambers, June 9, *My Utmost for His Highest* (Grand Rapids Michigan: Discovery House, 2015).

93   Catherine Marshall, *Moments That Matter* (Nashville, Tennessee: Thomas Nelson, 2001), 309.

Chapter Eight

94   Craig Anderson, *The Covenant Home Altar* (Chicago, IL: Covenant Publications, 2017), February 27.

95   Catherine Marshall, *Moments That Matter* (Nashville, Tennessee: Thomas Nelson, 2001), 281.

96   Priscilla Shirer, *Discerning the Voice of God* (Chicago, Illinois: Moody Publishers, 2012), 84.

97   Sarah Young, *Jesus Calling: Enjoying Peace in His Presence* (Nashville, Tennessee: Thomas Nelson, 2004), 23.

98   Mary Stevenson, *Footprints in the Sand,* (Hopewell, NJ: Ella H. Scharring-Hausen, Original publication unknown).

99   Dallas Willard, *Hearing God* (Downers Grove, Illinois: InterVarsity Press, 2012), 265.

100 Sarah Young, *Jesus Calling, Enjoying Peace in His Presence* (Nashville, Tennessee: Thomas Nelson, 2004), 90.

101 C. S. Lewis, *Letters to Malcom, Chiefly on Prayer* (San Francisco, CA: HarperOne, 2017).

102 John MacArthur, *Necessities for Effective Prayer* (sermon on January 23, 2011), https://**www.gty.org/**…/41-58/**the-necessities-for-effective-prayer.**

103 James Banks *Our Daily Bread* (Grand Rapids, Michigan: Our Daily Bread Ministries, 2017), November 6.

104 Oswald Chambers, July 4, *My Utmost for His Highest* (Grand Rapids, MI: Discovery House, 2015).

105 **Harvest Ministry,** *Trusting God for Daily Bread,* **(harvestministry.org/ muller).**

106 George Mueller, *Answers to Prayer* (Chicago: Moody Publishers, 2007), 35, 48.

107 Sarah Young, *Jesus Calling: Enjoying Peace in His Presence* (Nashville, Tennessee: Thomas Nelson, 2004), 75.

108 Kelly Wahlquist, *Catholicmom.com,* April 22, 2013, catholicmom. com/2013/04/22/until-god-opens-the-next-door-praise-him-in-the-hallway/.

109 Ibid.

110 Sarah Young, *Jesus Calling: Enjoying Peace in His Presence* (Nashville, Tennessee: Thomas Nelson, 2004), 184.

111 Ibid., 12.

112 Bill Hybels, *Too Busy Not to Pray* (Downers Grove, Illinois: InterVarsity Press, 1998), 88.

Chapter Nine

113 Catherine Marshall, *Moments That Matter* (Nashville, Tennessee: Thomas Nelson, 2001), 266.

114 Patricia Raybon, October 5, *God's Great Blessings* (Grand Rapids, Michigan: Tyndale House Publications, 2011).

115 Catherine Marshall, *Moments That Matter* (Nashville, Tennessee: Thomas Nelson, 2001), 113.

116 Ibid., 24.

117 Ibid., 139.

118 Laura Story, *Blessings,* (Brentwood, TN: INO records, 2011).

119 Catherine Marshall, *Moments That Matter* (Nashville, Tennessee: Thomas Nelson, 2001), 101.

120 J. I. Packer, *Knowing God* (Downers Grove, Illinois: InterVarsity Press, 1973), 71.

121 Hawk Nelson, *Diamonds,* Audio CD released March 17, 2015 (Brentwood, TN, Fair Trade Services, 2015).

122 J. I. Packer, *Knowing God* (Downers Grove, Illinois: InterVarsity Press, 1973), 227.

123 Catherine Marshall, *Moments That Matter* (Nashville, Tennessee: Thomas Nelson, 2001), 314.

124 J. I. Packer, *Knowing God* (Downers Grove, Illinois: InterVarsity Press, 1973), 224.

125 Dietrich Bonhoeffer, *Cost of Discipleship* (New York: Touchstone Books, 1995).

126 J. I. Packer, *Knowing God* (Downers Grove, Illinois: InterVarsity Press, 1973), 224.

127 Sarah Young, *Jesus Calling: Enjoying Peace in His Presence* (Nashville, Tennessee: Thomas Nelson, 2004), 7.

128 David Platt, *Radical* (New York: Multnomah Books, 1984), 173.

129 Catherine Marshall, *Moments That Matter* (Nashville, Tennessee: Thomas Nelson, 2001) 302.

130 Ibid.

131 J. I. Packer, *Knowing God* (Downers Grove, Illinois: InterVarsity Press, 1973), 96.

132 Sarah Young, *Jesus Calling: Enjoying Peace in His Presence* (Nashville, Tennessee: Thomas Nelson, 2004), 81.

133 Ibid.

134 Special thanks to Caleb Davison, a seminary student at Denver Seminary, for contributing this story.

135 Bill Hybels, *Too Busy Not to Pray* (Downers Grove, Illinois: InterVarsity Press, 1998), 10.

136 Catherine Marshall, *Moments That Matter* (Nashville, Tennessee: Thomas Nelson, 2001), 261.

137 Oswald Chambers, January 22, *My Utmost for His Highest* (Grand Rapids Michigan: Discovery House, 2015).

138 C. S. Lewis, *Problem of Pain* (San Francisco, CA: HarperOne, 2015).

139 Charles Stanley, *How to Listen to God* (Nashville, Tennessee: Thomas Nelson, 1985), 41.

140 Priscilla Shirer, *Discerning the Voice of God* (Chicago, Illinois: Moody Publishers, 2012), 85.

141 Doug Dameron, *Why Does God Allow Bad Things to Happen?* (Brighton, CO: Orchard Church: Reasonable Doubts Series, April 8, 2018).

142 David Platt, *Radical* (New York: Multnomah Books, 1984), 172.

143 J. I. Packer, *Knowing God* (Downers Grove, Illinois: InterVarsity Press, 1973), 86–87.

144 Dave Branon, *Our Daily Bread* (Grand Rapids, Michigan: Our Daily Bread Ministries, 2017), October 16.

145 Sarah Young, *Jesus Calling: Enjoying Peace in His Presence* (Nashville, Tennessee: Thomas Nelson, 2004), 55.

146 Ibid., 121.

147 Catherine Marshall, *Moments That Matter* (Nashville, Tennessee: Thomas Nelson, 2001), 331.

148 Thanks to Bernadette Pfeiffenberger for sharing this story from her blog.

149 Special thanks to Aaron Stern, Mills City Church, Ft. Collins, CO.

150 Oswald Chambers, May 14, *My Utmost for His Highest* (Grand Rapids Michigan: Discovery House, 2015).

151 Ibid., May 15.

152 Sarah Young, *Jesus Calling: Enjoying Peace in His Presence* (Nashville, Tennessee: Thomas Nelson, 2004), 218.

153 Oswald Chambers, May 19, *My Utmost for His Highest* (Grand Rapids Michigan: Discovery House, 2015).

154 Louie Giglio, *Indescribable* (Brentwood, TN: Dolby Digital, Sparrow Records, 2008).

Chapter Ten

155 Original author unknown, quoted on Facebook.com/700club/"i-believe-in-god-not/10154490015151668, September 29, 2016.

156 Oswald Chambers, June 10, *My Utmost for His Highest* (Grand Rapids Michigan: Discovery House, 2015).

157 Sir Roberts Anderson, *The Silence of God* (Grand Rapids, MI: Kregel Publications, 1942) 171, 206.

158 Dallas Willard, *Hearing God* (Downers Grove, Illinois: InterVarsity Press, 2012), 142.

159 Ibid., 256.

160 Priscilla Shirer, *Discerning the Voice of God* (Chicago, Illinois: Moody Publishers, 2012), 82.

161 Dallas Willard, *Hearing God* (Downers Grove, Illinois: InterVarsity Press, 2012), 146, 228–231, 219.

162 Doug Criss, CNN, accessed June 6, 2018, https://www.cnn.com/2018/06/04/us/jesse-duplantis-plane-new-message-trnd/index.html.

163 Sarah Young, *Jesus Calling: Enjoying Peace in His Presence* (Nashville, Tennessee: Thomas Nelson, 2004), 110.

Chapter Eleven

164 Elizabeth Elliot, *God's Guidance* (Grand Rapids, Michigan: Baker Book House, 1997), 42.

165 Catherine Marshall, *Moments That Matter* (Nashville, Tennessee: Thomas Nelson, 2001), 380.

166 Wesley C. Swanson, *Porch to Pulpit* (Wesley C. Swanson self-published, 2017).

167 Dallas Willard, *Hearing God* (Downers Grove, Illinois: InterVarsity Press, 2012), 256.

168 Special thanks to Colonel (RET) Al Shine for writing this story for me.

169 Oswald Chambers, March 28, *My Utmost for His Highest* (Grand Rapids Michigan: Discovery House, 2015).

170 Colton Jansen, *God Doesn't Call the Qualified...God Qualifies the Called* (LivingforJesus.com, August 23, 2011).

171 Ibid.

172 Used by special permission of Joe and Peggy Valentino.

Chapter Twelve

173 Oswald Chambers, January 31, *My Utmost for His Highest* (Grand Rapids, MI: Discovery House, 2015).

174 Ibid., May 30.

175 Ibid., February 28.

176 Dallas Willard, *Hearing God* (Downers Grove, Illinois: InterVarsity Press, 2012), 266.

177 Ibid., 267.

178 Oswald Chambers, *My Utmost for His Highest* (Grand Rapids Michigan: Discovery House, 2015), May 25.

179 Ibid., June 3.

180 Charles Stanley, *How to Listen to God* (Nashville, Tennessee: Thomas Nelson, 1985), 56.

Chapter Thirteen

181 John Muir, quoted by Samuel Hall Young in *Alaska Days with John Muir* (CreateSpace Independent Publishing Platform, 2015).

182 Elizabeth Elliot, *God's Guidance* (Grand Rapids, Michigan: Baker Book House, 1997), 85.

CPSIA information can be obtained
at www.ICGtesting.com
Printed in the USA
LVHW091734140819
627629LV00006B/937/P

9 781642 792362